CW00494275

About the Author

The author came to England at the age of twelve and struggled to complete secondary education. He did, however, find inspiration and developed a love of reading, literature and biographies. Through arts, music and drama he experienced the power of performance on TV, theatre and radio and successfully ran a few family businesses, held a few management positions, became a financial advisor and is a retired driving instructor. He found answers, direction and purpose of life from divine revelations, experienced happiness and contentment in the remembrance of the Creator. A great desire for knowledge remains even now at sixty and a grandfather.

Towards Understanding Yourself

Amjad Saleem Ramzan

Towards Understanding Yourself

Olympia Publishers
London

www.olympiapublishers.com
OLYMPIA PAPERBACK EDITION

A CIP catalogue record for this title is available from the British Library.

ISBN: 978-1-84897-883-6

First Published in 2017

Olympia Publishers
60 Cannon Street
London
EC4N 6NP

Printed in Great Britain

Dedication

This book is dedicated to my mother, Safia. Despite her sad and traumatic life of eighty-five years, her submission to God's will and strong faith in Allah, has never wavered.

And

Also to a very special, loving and supporting wife, Salma, who also has strong faith.

CONTENTS

Read in the name of your lord who has created all that exists[1].
He created man from a clot (a piece of thick coagulated blood)[2].

We all act and behave according to our learning and experiences. Correct knowledge is the key to understanding life.

Divine message is a blessing, its faith and practice can bring peace and harmony to the body and soul.

---

[1] Quran (96:1)
[2] Quran (96:2)

Foreword

The mystery of self has fascinated man throughout the ages. Understanding one's self is probably the greatest intellectual challenge of human beings. Early psychologists attempted to define the self in various ways. One basic definition relies on the physical body as the boundary between the self and others. Today's popular conception of self has evolved into three dimensions: the individual self, which is defined as differentiation from others, the relational self, referring to assimilation with others, and the collective self, achieved by inclusion into larger social groups. This perspective is functional in understanding the individual interaction with others. This approach excludes the spiritual self and the presence of soul as it lacks the complexity and the richness or the experience of the spiritual inner world. We all have the options to seek knowledge, that can help us to have a better and a clearer understanding of self – self to believe in our creator, and to have faith in life. This can help us to bring happiness, peace and contentment to our inner self.

Self-awareness has also been critically studied in psychology and philosophy. Our self-awareness plays the key part in making decisions which determines the outcome of our actions. Self-awareness can be empowering because it can reveal our strength and weakness. To understand the things we do, what we say and why we say it, we may need to understand the internal process of our emotions, which prompt our actions and reactions. For better understanding of self-awareness some key areas need to be assessed which would include our faith, personal values, personality traits, habits and physiological needs that drive our behaviour. This contributes to the manifesting of our personality.

Now, in our age new fascinating Tomography scans are able to show which part of the brain is active during different tasks. The occipital cortex in the back of the brain contains the visual area and is stimulated by sight. The superior temporal cortex contains the auditory area, which is activated by hearing. The insula and motor cortex contain the speech centre of the brain, which are stimulated by speaking. In fact cross sections of the motor area of the brain indicates which area control which part of body, like our eyes, ears, torso, shoulder, elbow, wrist, hand, fingers, neck, face, lips, tongue, hip, knee, ankle and toes.

Where we carry out our thought processes and how is our conscience formed in our brain, are searching questions which still remain a mystery.

Millions of nerve impulses generated in the brain per second produce an electrical field that can be measured to produce a reading known as electro-encephalogram (EEG) which show different wave patterns depending on the activity level of brain, when it is awake, relaxed, meditating or in creative thought.

Most of us believe there is a spirit in our body, our soul, which when it leaves our body we are pronounced dead. We may never be able to physically locate our soul, our intuitions, or our thoughts, because these are not physical properties.

These experiences remain elusive to the microscope for a scientific analysis.

Knowledge is drawn from, history, nature and revelations. For a better understanding of inner-selves we should look towards our creator. Only our maker can provide the answers that can lead us to having a better understanding of our inner self. Our creator, God, integrated our soul into our body. These answers are in the divine revelations, the true knowledge from our originator. Since the creation of Adam, every living soul has had a purpose in life. To guide mankind, God sent messengers and prophets to every civilization, the divine message has always been the same to believe in the one true God our creator. Many ancient civilizations rejected the revelations, defied the truth and mocked the prophets. Our creator draws our attention to monuments left by those ignorant people who reject the truth; we have the choice to learn from their mistakes. The last book of revelations, the Holy Quran, it is nothing but the truth that has provided all the answers.

This book can help the reader to achieve a better and cleared understanding of self, mind, body and spirit. It provides answers and helps the reader towards self-improvement and personal growth. It will also prepare the reader with true knowledge which can bring discipline, order, and help establish faith in self and in God, and a strong foundation to deal with many trials and tribulations of this life. Many of the answers will also help the reader to achieve peace and contentment in this life and success in the hereafter.

Self

Our physical self portrays a kind of image to the observer. If you could ask him/her to describe "you" they can only refer to their own direct experiences or what they have come to know of you. If we are asked to introduce our self, we confirm our physical presence with our personal detail and remind the listener of our common connection – the human relationship that binds us in time. If we are asked about our personal self, what is it that makes us a unique individual? We would refer to our personal values, believes, achievements, goals, aspirations and our personal experiences. If we are asked about our inner "self ", our self-awareness, our conscience or spirit- or soul, we can only respond to these self-searching questions correctly if we have knowledge. Throughout human history, man has been impressed with his own achievements by using his sense perceptions with cognition to learn of the world around him, leaving him very pleased with his own ability to manipulate and take control of some of the physical world around him for his immediate needs.

As for the soul in his body which has not taken any physical shape or form, it cannot be manipulated or controlled easily, it has always been beyond the common grasp. In order to understand it, without truth of knowledge, over the centuries there have been many misunderstandings in different cultures and religions. The soul of the human body actually forms self-awareness. It may be hard to comprehend or to accept this, as it is often the case with us humans. Things which cannot be seen in a physical form may cast doubts and scepticism in our minds; indeed we are not always ready to accept the unseen over which we have no control. This can be the case, especially if our objective and contentious mind creates its own dilemma by not acknowledging the presence of "spirit' in our body. Some of us may continue to deny its presence or its actual source and origin. This would be our decision, a result of exercising our freedom of choice. It can also be considered as our own personal view formed with our own free will. Before an action can be ascribed to a free will, three following conditions need to be satisfied. Firstly, the agent must have been able to do otherwise. The act must originate in the agent and not in some external forces and the act must be the outcome of rational deliberation. To deliberate we need the correct information and sound knowledge. In the case of the soul, the source would be its creator and its knowledge would be in the form of divine revelations.

To give an example of our acceptance of the unseen we must consider the Internet waves that work our mobile phones. Can we actually see the sound signals transmitting to our mobile phones?

(It only indicates that the reception of signal is possible.)

We know our mobile transmits and receives signals. We are ready to accept the transmissions' presences when our mobile is working.

When we see our own reflection in the mirror, our eyes transmit the information to our brain, our soul together with our memory confirms that it is in fact our own reflection. The transmission of the information to and from the brain can be monitored but this is not the case for the soul.

The human body is an intensively researched subject that still has many secrets to divulge. Techniques to visualize living cells are being perfected and new chemicals and receptors are being discovered on a daily basis. Each new finding acts as a stepping-stone to the next discovery.

Modern science continues in its quest to treat the many illnesses of the human body, and it continues to make positive progress always finding new treatments, discovering better methods and finding more effective solutions. Science is always finding new techniques, continuously in preparations to meet new challenges to treat human illness; it is forever always in pursuit of excellence. Yet for these leaps, science is still unable to locate or provide any physical proof of a human soul in a body.

In fact, the scientists still fail to agree on the spirit or soul's presence in us, which actually enables us to exercise our free will. Scientists are increasingly uncomfortable in accepting its connection with its originator and our creator. The connection of the soul to divine entity and its independence of the body have been most difficult for some to comprehend. To modern science, our joys, our sorrows, our memories and our ambitions, our sense of personal identity and free will, are in fact no more than the behaviour of a vast assembly of nerve cells and their associated molecules, a pack of neurons as described by the codiscoverer of the DNA structure Francis Crick (1916-2004)[3]. In his book, Crick argued that the spectacular advances of modern science make the concepts of soul and consciousness redundant. When most people are asked what they would consider the essence of their life they would refer to the 'self' because of their private and personal experiences and beliefs, who act and interact in a coherent and purposeful way with the environment. The existence of such feeling begs the question, where does the 'self' come from? What gives us the power to experience ourselves as consistent entities with goals and values? Even stronger, what gives us the power to think, to have a mind? This is arguably the biggest conceptual issue is psychology. How do the brain and the mind relate to each other? This issue is known as the mind and brain problem. There are three different views of interaction between mind and brain. The first is the oldest and intuitively the most appealing. It says that the mind (or the soul) is something independent of the body. This view is called dualism. The second approach states that the mind is nothing but a by-product of the biological processes taking place in a particular brain. This view is called materialism. The third approach says that the mind is indeed realised in a brain but it could be copied to any other brain, just like information on a computer can be copied to other machines. This is the

---

[3] In 1954, James Watson and Francis Crick announced they had found "the secret of life", the quastructure of deoxyribonucleic acid, or DNA.

functionalist view. Scientists feel increasingly uncomfortable with the dualistic view with the emphasis religion had placed on the immortality of the soul, and the connection of the soul to a divine entity and its independence of the body. At the same time, they are unwilling to reduce the human mind to nothing but brain tissue, so that in practice most defend some kind of implicit dualist view. It gives humans free will, because in the dualist view consciousness is the centre of the mind, nothing happens unless it is licensed by the mind. This puts humans in full control over their decisions and actions. They can choose their course of action from a number of alternatives, a phenomenon that is referred to as free will. They are guided by reason and try to achieve different goals. Having free will also means that the individual is held responsible for their actions; simply having the option to choose enables them to choose freely.

In 1954 James Watson and Francis Crick announced that they had found "the secret of life" the structure of deoxyribonucleic acid, or DNA. Exactly fifty years later the complete sequence of the human genome was published, pointing exactly where each of our 20,000-25,000 genes are positioned within our 46 chromosomes. While researchers originally predicted that everyone's DNA would be 99.9% identical, analysis of the individual genomes now suggests that at least 44% of our genes have variations. These variations dictate not only the colour of our eyes and skin, but also whether our hair is curly or straight, amongst many other features.

The following pages also support the dualist view. Dualism has an intuitive appeal because it puts conscious information processing at the centre of our functioning as it gives us the feeling of being in control of our actions.

To date, science has not been able to physically locate a soul in a body. Since the beginning of time, human beings have continued to put forward their own interpretations on the properties of the human soul. This may be because they have poor knowledge, biased views, due to laziness or ignorance. This may well continue until the end of time if one chooses to ignore the presence of soul in the body and its integration by its creator. If we are in search for the truth, we cannot ignore the knowledge given to us by the infinite source - our creator - the true knowledge provided to us in the form of divine revelations.

As the sultan of saints, Shaikh Abd Al Qadir Al-Jilani in the 'Sublime Revelation' pointed out in one of his discourses, "The person who suffers real privation, is he who is deprived of the lord of truth, Allah (Almighty and glorious is he) and who misses the opportunity of nearness to him in this world and the hereafter. Allah, Almighty and Glorious, has said in one of his books, **"Oh son of Adam, if I escape you, everything has escaped you."**

"So when I have fashioned him completely and breather into him (Adam) the soul I created for him, then fall (you) down, prostrating yourself unto him." (Quran 15:29)

"By Adam and him who perfected him in proportion." (Quran 92:7)

"Then he showed him what is wrong for him and what is right for him." (Quran 92:8)

"And indeed we have created man; we know what his own self whispers to him. We are nearer to him than his jugular vein (by our knowledge). (Quran 50:16)

A miracle from Allah to his prophet Mohammed peace be upon him

"And this Quran is not such as could ever be produced by other than Allah (Lord of the heavens and the earth) , but it is a confirmation of (the revelation) which was before it (i.e. the Torah and the Gospel) and a full explanation of the book (i.e. laws decreed for mankind) – wherein there is no doubt from the Lord of mankind, Jinn and all that exists "[4]

Note. The prophet Mohammed, peace be upon him, was born 29th April 571 AD. He died at age of 63. He said, There was no prophet among the prophets but was given miracles because of which people had security or had belief, but what I have been given is the divine revelation which Allah has revealed to me. So I hope that my followers will be more than those of any other prophet on the day of resurrection. Sahih Al-Bukhari, 9/7274.

[4] Quran (10;37)

Know thy Self

"Know thy self," was first uttered by one of the wise men of the ancient Greeks.

This commandment was originally inscribed in the Holy Scriptures as a part of a divine guidance to man. According to (Qur'an 2.30 Bible, Gen 1:26-28) according to these religious texts, the human being is the "Vicegerent on earth" a representative of God. Therefore, in order to fulfil his responsibility, first it requires the individual to realize his own self to attain his own true potential. The importance was given to understand one's inner self, it was one of the prime messages preached and practiced by all the prophets. Over the centuries, this divine message was conveyed by the prophets to guide each civilization. It is for the benefit of all mankind. It begins with the desire to know our inner-self. A good starting point would be with our awareness of us as being a part of the creation on this planet. Earth is one of many planets in our solar system that orbits a central star, the Sun. The orbit of each planet varies based on its distance from the Sun. The Earth has a single moon, the most conspicuous object in the night sky. Our planet's distance from the sun is perfectly placed, it creates a unique atmosphere and temperature, has its own laws of gravity that sustains all forms of life. This is very noticeable from space by its distinctive thin blue line, this perfectly arranged atmosphere with its own environment designed for human existence along with millions of different kinds of species by the divine creator and the origination of the whole cosmos.

In the following revelation, Allah reminds man to reflect and understand his great favour to all mankind of his great creation

It is not for the sun to overtake the moon, nor does the night outstrip the day. The all float, each in an orbit. (36.40)

It is He who makes the sun a shining thing and the moon a light and measured out for it stages that you might know the number of years and the reckoning. Allah did not create this but in truth. He explains the Ayat (proofs, evidences, verses, revelations) in detail for people who have knowledge. (10:5)

We human beings are the only creation blessed with conscious awareness. At some stage in our life of existence, we can easily be tempted to wonder, and ask the two very important questions.

Why was this world created? What is the purpose of our life on this earth?

For a moment, one should stop to reflect on one's current state in time and pause to examine their inward push, that drives them forward with energy and force to have more and improve on what they have for their uncertain life span. For some of us it may be more appropriate to have a better understanding of self and make time to understand our conscious state and our inner self. Wherever we may be, whatever status we may have in society, whatever possessions we may have, we are conscious and we always have our inner self. Our Self-awareness is empowering, a closer study and recognition of it can reveal our areas of weaknesses, which may be causing us a problem. A close examination of our inner self can guide and help us to improve our psychological needs and give strength to improve our weak performances. A better understanding of our inner self can also increase our motivations, which can help us to accomplish our tasks with better results. If we make attempts to understand our inner self better, we may come to realise, that actually our first duties are to ourselves, our first feeling is contained in our self, and our instincts are dedicated to our natural self-preservations. We can try to know our self; we owe it ourselves to seek and search for the truth. It would be better for us to make it as a rule of this life. As humans we endeavour to discover every new life form in the deepest depths of the oceans, man is continuously in pursuit with relentless efforts to find new life on other planets millions of light years away.

We need to be sincere and ask how much effort we really put in to discovering our inner self. What could possibly be more important than understanding one's self and to discover the world that can be found from within and in realising its great potential in connecting with its creator, which can bring great change to us and a real positive transformation in us.

This course of action may provide us with the satisfaction we may be longing for. This may fulfil the emptiness that we may have experienced despite all our material wealth, fame, and all worldly achievements. The powerful status, worldwide fame, all the acclaims and all the recognitions and praise that we may have temporally enjoyed , all of which will be left behind when we close our eyes to this world for ever, never to return in any form.

The direct enjoyments of our achievements will stop when the physical self is no more.

As long as we breathe, our body benefits in some way from our positive/negative actions and achievements. For those who believe, the soul does not perish when they die, it passes to an intermediary state called Barkzaa, where it continues to benefit from the positive/negative action of its courier, this assurance is given by its creator.

A subject which I hope to provide more information on in the latter chapters of this book.

Self-Awareness

Self-awareness is the explicit understanding that one exists as an individual with one's private thoughts and conscious experience. To become more self-aware we can look at the key areas that make up our personality traits, our values, habits, convictions, and psychological needs that drive our behaviours, emotions and our actions.

Nature has installed in our minds an insatiable desire to seek the truth and create order in our life. In being conscious, we are aware of our thoughts, our sense perception, our different moods, emotions and dreams. It would appear that we have access to the inner mind, which is the core of our individual being, and that there is nothing in the world that we are on more intimate terms with than our self. Yet this self remains the elusive object of knowledge and understanding.

Illusion and self-deception may stand in the way of an honest, penetrating and fearless self-appraisal. The fact is that we are created as self-conscious and self-regarding beings. Some of us may need to have a better understanding of our consciousness and how it is formed. What is the fine quality of self-awareness in a man that sparks and ignites the process of self-accountability, which inspires him to have a love for great ideas and provides continuous support for his achievements?

Our creator has pointed out that a person's personality can be the highest product of the whole cosmos.

A fundamental difference between a man and an animal is that while an animal only knows, feels and thinks, a man not only knows and feels but is also conscious and thinks, in other words, whilst an animal is only conscious. Human beings are self-conscious.

O mankind! We have created you from male and female and made you into nations and tribes that you may know one another. Verily, the most honourable of you with Allah is that believer who has At-Taqua (the pious, most God-fearing). Verily, Allah is all knowing, all aware. (50:13)

It is this fact that creates all the difference that there is between the nature of an animal and a human being. This self-consciousness seed has not evolved from the evolutionary process or by the amazing power of our brain cells or our body's chemistry. It is the wonder of the great creator, the originator. Sometimes our philosophical points of view help us to explain our feelings and emotions. Science is able to monitor our brain's activity and provide proof for most human experiences and illnesses. We use the more suitable of the two to report our findings. Philosophy tries to explain the result, whereas most of the time science is able to verify the truth. However, science is still unable to provide any psychological explanations for our subjective experiences, of enjoying a beautiful garden or a beautiful sunset. Subjective refers to feelings and an experience that depends on the individual's own particular viewpoint and traits. A subjective claim cannot be proved right or wrong by any generally accepted criteria. This self-awareness is our real experience; it's as real to us as our existence. Our bodies physically alter from being young to old as the experience of self-consciousness grows. This self-consciousness, I, remains the same age from young to old in sickness and health, single or married .

Only human beings make promises, there would be no expectation of future obligation if we as individuals didn't have our self-consciousness. If I were a wholly physical matter, a human being wouldn't be capable of making free choices. As human beings, we are an entity which contains in itself all the aspects of biological, social, cultural, economic, spiritual, and mystical attributes. These aspects do contribute to some extent in the manifestation of our behaviour of our self, and can add traits to our personality. Our every action is witnessed by our self, our conscious awareness - our soul – spirit, it is all connected and stems from the same root base. These were interlinked and were integrated from their inception by our creator – God. This 'I', our self-consciousness, is linked to our spirit.

To form an opinion, make a choice or decide, we need information. Sometimes the information is through a subjective experience and at times in being objective. Our feelings and opinions help our consciousness to form a bond, our compass, our touchstone that our inner self begins to trust. Our very own personal belief, our self-consciousness, which intuitively becomes our initial choice.

This all results from our learning and understanding, which is all based from the knowledge we have gained. The knowledge we consciously acquired will enabled us to make a free choice.

To believe and have faith in our creator is a freedom of choice. The right choice can only be made from the correct knowledge and information. The correct choice can/will bring a change providing a better clearer understanding – will push for a real improvement, which will inspire the self and ignite the spark for a positive transformation, this can take the acquiring personality to new heights.

In order to understand the" I" in ourselves, this Holy Spirit, our soul, we need to first be free from laziness, prejudice, preconceptions, doubtful, incorrect or impartial influences. First is to have a free and open mind and make a real effort to gain the knowledge from the Holy Scriptures which are indisputed. The provide us with the correct information and explanations which are directly from the source and the creator of our soul, the originator the omnipotent – God- regarding our soul , the revelation states, ***"So when I have fashioned him completely and breathed into him (Adam) the soul which I created for him, then fall (you) down prostrating yourselves unto him." (15:29).***[5]

In this busy and proactive life, we may need to give some priority to our personal aims and desires. Our physical health always takes priority, we may need to give some importance to gaining the knowledge from the Holy Scriptures only then can we begin to understand, learn and fully appreciate the truth. Only the Holy Scriptures can provide us with all the true guidance in the right direction which can lead us to have a

[5] Quran (91:8)

better understanding of self and human nature, which is guided by the 'I', the soul.

My exhausting inquires have led me to find that only the Holy Qur'an has completely remained in its original form. This will remain so until the end of all life on earth. This assurance has been provided in the Holy Qur'an by its author God.

In the well-established archaeological records, the Arabic script goes back to the fourth century AD. These indicate that the Arabic script evolved from Nabatean, a direct descendant of Aramaic which itself is an offspring of a proto-Semitic alphabet.

Arabic as we know it today, developed from the language of the Quraysh (The Prophet Mohammed's tribe) the purest and the best evolved of the north Arabian dialects. Today, it is the most widely used Semitic tongue, surpassing all others in its wealth of synonyms, harmonious patterns, concision, clarity and eloquence.

The Arabic alphabet is simple and concise. It has twenty-eight letters, all consonants, with the exception of three used for long vowels. The other vowels are supplied by fourteen diacritical marks which also serve as noun and verb modifiers. These are placed above or below the consonants to bring out the correct pronunciation of the words.

The Arabic script remains the second most widely used alphabetic writing in the world. Besides Arabic, over ten languages retain the Arabic script, the most important being Urdu, Persian, Pushto, Kurdish, Sindhi and Punjabi. Three hundred million people use it as a mother tongue and over eight hundred million to read the Holy Quran, it has immortalised the Arabic language and script. Over the past few centuries many other scripts have been used by man, Arabic of the Holy Quran will remain until the end of time.

The Holy Quran has a total of six thousand, six hundred and six verses, which makes seventy thousand words. These were revealed in parts over a period of twenty-three years.

Across the world today, due to literary styles and punctuations, the copies of the Holy Quran may appear different at a glance. Sometime due to pronunciation and local dialect may even sound different, BUT the words remain the same as the original revelations. Sometimes, because of its translation from the Arabic to other languages, the meanings of the words are not always the same in every language, there the scholars may differ on a particular word meaning.

The following revelations have stood as true testament through time and will remain so until the end of time. Even upon revelation, the Quran was met with opposition and doubt, this too will remain until the end of time as these are reactions of human nature.

This is the book (the Qural-Muttaqun (the pious believers of Islamic Monotheism who fear Allah much (abstain from all kinds of sins and evil deeds which he has forbidden) and love Allah much (perform all kinds of good deeds which he has ordained). 2:2

A revelation from Allah the Most Gracious the Most Merciful. 41:2

A Book whereof the verses are explained in detail, a Quran in Arabic for people who know. 41:3

Verily, we, it is we who have sent down the Quran and surely we will guard it from corruption. 15:9

And thus we have sent to you (O Mohammed) Ruh (a revelation and a mercy) of our command. You know not Quran, a light wherewith we guide whosoever of our slaves we will. And verily you (O Mohammed) are indeed guiding mankind to the straight path. (i.e. Allah's religion of Islamic Monotheism). 42:52

Say O Mohammed, "O mankind! Verily I sent to you all as the messenger of Allah, to whom he belongs, the dominion of the heavens and earth. (None has the right to be worshipped but He). It is He who gives life and causes death. So believe in Allah and his Messenger Muhammed the prophet who can neither read nor write, Muhammed who believes in Allah and his words this Quran, the Torah and the Gospel and also Allah's word 'Be' and he was Jesus, son of Mary, and follow him so that you may be guided. 7:158

Had we sent down this Quran on a mountain, you would surely have seen it humbling itself and rent asunder by the fear of Allah. Such are the parables which we put forward to mankind that they may reflect. 59:21

And if you (Arab, pagans, Jews and Christians) are in doubt concerning that which We have sent down (the Quran) to our slave (Mohammed) then bring Surah (chapter) of the like thereof and call your witnesses (supporters and helpers) besides Allah, if you're truthful. 2.23

Say, (O Mohammed), if mankind and the Jinn were together to produce the like of this Quran, they could not produce the like thereof, even if they helped one another. 17:88

Do they not consider the Quran carefully? Had it been from other than Allah, they would surely have found many contradictions. 4:82

Move not your tongue concerning the Quran, O Mohammed to make haste therewith. 75:16

It is for us to collect and to give you. O Mohammed) the ability to recite it, the Quran. 75:17

And when we have recited it to you O Mohammed through Jibrail, then follow its recitations. 75:18

Then it is for us (Allah) to make it clear to you. 75:19

We shall make you recite the Quran so you Mohammed shall not forget it. 87:6

Except what Allah may will. He knows what is apparent and what is hidden. 87:7

The revelation of the Quran was a miracle, fourteen hundred years ago, in which it states the origin and creation of man.

Then we made the Nutah into a clot (a piece of thick, coagulated blood), then We made the clot into a little lump of flesh, then We made out of the little lump flesh and bones, then We clothed the bones with flesh, and We brought it forth as another creation. So blessed in Allah, the Best of creators. 23:14

Only now in the recent past has science been able to establish the true sequence of events that occur inside the womb. It is up to us to think, reflect and choose, or live by our own conjectures.

The holy Quran's preservation is guaranteed by God, God the creator of the whole universe, the lord of the ever-expanding universe, the lord of the whole cosmos. The Qur'an in which there is no doubt. It is the custodian of all laws the preserver of all the revelation. This was revealed little over fourteen hundred years ago to his last prophet Mohammed (pbuh) who is a prophet to all mankind. "According to the Holy Qur'an the last book of revelation to Prophet Mohammed (pbuh) in which God states regarding origin and the formation and the creation of man and his soul. It is up to us to accept the truth and reflect on the facts provided or choose to live by our own conjectures.

Soul (Spirit)

The Prophet said the most excellent holy war is that for the conquest of the self.

What is this entity? It is not something material. We cannot physically locate it. It is within us. It is a part of us, we hear, we see, we experience. One of the first things God created was intellect and intellect needs a courier. A conveyance which is our body, it is by the means of soul man is lord of the creation. It is by the means of soul, man acquires knowledge of God. It is by this spirit he begins to understand God's creations and learn to appreciate God's attributes. It is by the means of soul he finds nearness to his creator. It is the soul that is asked and rebuked and rewarded by its creator. Our soul's food is knowledge. Our soul is the king over our body. Our limbs are its servants and they only obey its commands.

The spirit's presence should be acknowledged within us. This particle of divine light, this atom of divinity, if neglected, will become dim with the passage of time. If we lose balance, and wholly pursue our desires and passions, we will become slaves to our bodies and its carnal desires. Thus this self will remain nothing but breathing clay matter. When man does not ask of his soul, he is forgetful of his creator, he does not know himself, only when you know yourself you know your creator.

In some cases, our egoistic tendencies impede the progress of our souls towards higher virtues and hence some of us go to the length of denying the possibility of its existence.

When the soul is cleansed and purified, it finds contentment and peace. Soul is the recipient of divine light, our intuition, our inspiration with which a dark and dormant mind can be illuminated with the spark of divine guidance, can begin to take effect; soul inspires man to move forward, to gain, to acquire, and to achieve in what he wants to believe.

The prophet Mohammed (pbuh) was once asked what is spirit he replied,

"And they ask you (O Muhammad) concerning the spirit Say : the spirit is one of the things , the knowledge of which is only with my lord .And of knowledge, you (mankind) have been given only a little " [6]

English translation in the Noble Quran by Dr Muhammed Muhsun Khan, Dr Mohammed Taqi ud di Hilai (page 355).

The prophet Mohammed (pbuh) is also reported to have stated that soul is breathed into the embryo forty days after fertilization takes place and at death, a person's spirit or soul doesn't perish, it is extracted from the body and enters a intermediate state known as Barkzah which is a parallel universe, which no human has ever seen before, it is immaterial. This stage results in a cold sleep slumber where they will rest until judgement day. The interrogation by the angels takes place with everyone who dies, no matter whether he is buried in the grave or cremated or his body is

---

[6] Quran (17:85)

immersed in the river or eaten up by carnivorous birds and animals. The human soul is a kind of combination of the heart, spirit, and passion of a person. According to the Holy Scriptures, the divine sanctified soul finds true contentment in remembering its creator. Man finds peace and harmony in fulfilling his obligations to his creator in worship and also with all his sincere actions in earning his daily bread, leading his life of integrity and honesty with all humans and showing love and compassion to all of God's creations simply by following the set examples of all the prophets. The spiritual saints who have followed the prophets' instructions and have put in practice the prophets' teachings into their lives and are devoted to worship of their creator. They have had the experiences of divine illuminations. They have stated that the experiences are not just limited to the prophets. It is open to everyone. Which they have reported, can be achieved with total submission to the creator, with continued worship reaching the stages of certain apex of noble piety. That purifies the heart and sanctifies the soul. In the lives of spiritual saints the love of this world does not exists, for them, there is constant passionate longing of their soul to be with its creator. **Indeed, he succeeds who purifies his own self (and obeys and performs all that Allah ordered) Quran 91:9.** They describe the human soul as a divine thing not belonging to the sensual world but the spiritual world. They report that the human soul is divine in nature and it contains three principles. Firstly, nature of the soul is intellectual, which is its true self, which can be the highest self to be identified with the heart and spirit of a man. This is divine in its origin. Secondly, the reasoning soul, this represents the normal human life. That is the reproachful soul which resonates with normal human beings in whom the voice of conscience is at work, to correct the downward pull of the flesh. Thirdly, the animal soul which is irrational in nature, the headstrong soul which is under the control of animal nature, When our feeling take charge, our emotions and our physical needs give rise to many kinds of notions to the inner self, which we experience in the seat of our hearts and in the core of our minds. There can be many kinds of notions, sometimes of a selfish nature, and a passionate nature, for vanity, for show, for lust, or evil and vengeful or pure angelic nature. Sometimes our actions are not only hasty and bold. They are based on impulse alone and often without fear of grave consequences. When there is no thought given to our actions or consequences, we act and behave in a manner as if we are blind – this can amount to ignorance. The result of which not only becomes a personal embarrassment, very often impulsive and emotional behaviour leads to disaster which can bring lasting pain and suffering. In such cases, we must be true to ourselves – and to our soul and humbly accept the failure was due to our own self. We may have failed to maintain the balance and control over our body and soul. We may have given more importance to our physical and mental desires and neglected the presence of the soul, and have truly failed to draw benefit from our soul through its partnership with our body. All faculties of man must relate to his spirit, his will, his choice, his sense of proportion, his imagination, and consciousness in respect of good and evil. We are all blessed with the capacity to learn and to seek the benefit with our own efforts. It is our human obligation to learn and acquire knowledge to have a better understanding of self and our spirit. Our learning will help us to make the right decision, an intelligent a virtuous decision, if we do not have the knowledge to deal with a situation, we feel vulnerable, unprepared and remain open to all kinds of perils and unpleasant surprises. This may lead to us feeling helpless and alone; this may push us further into a negative state of mind without hope or sense of direction and utter confusion that can drive us into depths of despair. We need to reflect and examine our own present state. We may have neglected to provide our soul its true requirements of knowledge, and may have failed to develop a connection with its creator. Our efforts in purifying our soul can achieve a direct benefit to experience pure intuition and inspirations. Our spirit and its natural link with our creator can provide support to us for the many trials and the tribulations of this sometimes very difficult life. When we believe in our creator with resolute faith and with practice of religious knowledge, only then we may receive true guidance through our intuition. These will all depend on the knowledge, learning and practice of our faith in God. The true and correct knowledge acquired and understood with practice can only bring true and lasting comfort to the restless inner self and soul. Dependent on the degree of belief and firmness of faith, only with the resolute faith will we experience the satisfactions and feel an intimate closeness with God. At the time of death, many questions come to mind and explanations are asked for, why this and why that? A certain amount of comfort and understanding can be drawn; it only comes to the resolute heart and purified soul. God sent us a prophet to set perfect examples to follow in life. He created all of nature for our benefit. He has inspired man to make all kinds of new discoveries. Only he can provide contentment to a soul, every moment spent on this earth can be rewarded. For the knowledge of self, we must look to its creator. To fully appreciate our creator, self and body we need to make efforts to achieve a better understanding of our mind body and spirit.

The great Persian poet, Rumi,[7] who had great insight of mystical experience wrote the following couplet in his book The Mathnawi of Jalaludddin Rumi

"Sense perception is captive in the intellect."

"O readers know also intellect in captive to spirit

He also wrote the following;

In as much as this body is the abode (nest) of (these) four dispositions, they are named the four mischief-seeking birds.

The four immaterial birds which infest their way have made their home in the hearts of people. There is the duck, the peacock, the crow and the cock; these are a parable of four (evil) dispositions in (human) souls. The duck is greed, and the cock is lust; eminence is like the peacock and crow is worldly desire. The crow's object of desire is this, that he forms hopes and wishes for immortality or long life. The duck

---

[7] . Rumi's-*The Masnavi,* his famous work of six volumes, are 25,700 verses – Persian poetry mostly inspired by true Islamic hadiths and the holy Quran.

is greed, for her bill is always in the ground, seeking what is buried in the wet and dry. But the true believer from his confidence is that divine life, conducts his take, his allotted portions of worldly goods, in a leisurely manner and with deliberation."

The Human Brain

In this section, some information is provided for the reader to gain a better understanding of the human brain and some of its functions. How it controls and manipulates the many complex organs of the human body. Also further information on how an embryo splits, develops and part of it forms the brain, its contribution to intellect, to memories, to emotions and to the limbic system that controls subconscious, instinctive behaviour related to survival as well as our moods.

At birth, a baby's brain contains over 200 billion brain cells – as many stars as there in the Milky Way. Each brain cell is wired to its neighbours through up to 20,000 different branches resulting in trillions of connections, more than the number of stars in the universe.

The human brain is the most complex organism in the entire world. Each of the billions of nerve cells within our brain form connections between 1,000 and 20,000 other neurons. The possible routes an electrical impulse can take through our brain is therefore astronomically large and measured in the trillion of trillions. It is these connections that facilitate some of the higher functions of the brain, the aspects that make us uniquely human, including intelligence, consciousness and personality.

Many of the human experiences and emotions appear to result from many interactions of brain and body responses.

Many different parts of the brain are involved in processing emotions. In the human brain, the brainstem is one of the hardest working areas of the brain. It initiates and coordinates the hundreds of subconscious body processes that enable body functions. The brainstem is situated under the cerebrum and leads into the top of the spinal cord. All nerve signals into and out of brain from every part of the body pass through the brainstem. All of which is not simply by accident or chance but by unique design by its creator, God. Our creator reminds us that from a drop of sperm an embryo is formed, from this the **formation** of the human brain begins. The brain has its own life span, a human brain that will form its own identity, which empowers a really unique individual. We praise and salute the scientists who continue in their endeavours to bring us new discoveries .They are always enhancing our understanding. Their discoveries are continuous; their endeavours are remarkable; it is all achieved by using their brains. We are always full of praise and admiration for them. We envy their scientific findings, some experts have dedicated the entire life in pursuit of answers.

I have put together some information in order to help the reader to achieve and have a better understanding of the formation of the human brain. This is not an attempt to provide complete information on the brain which is a mammoth task in itself, (a complete volume would be needed) which would require input from many scientists; some aspects would still remain a mystery for all of us.

[8]"The fabric of brain was discovered in the last 150 years. The formation of the brain starts as a slab of cells in the upper layer of the embryo, which become irreversibly different from other cells about three weeks from its gestation. Different parts are already designated to form specific relations with the body in the future. Both the brain and body of the embryo have bilateral symmetry but hidden difference exists between left and right halves. Brain and spinal cord roll into a hollow cylinder, then in a few days, cell multiplication occurs round the central cavity, and cells migrate outwards to form rudimentary brain nuclei in the wall of the tube. Some cells become neurones and others change into non-neural support cell(glia) Ventral cells in brainstem and cord grow axons out the muscles of the trunk, limbs and viscera after four weeks, the anterior most motor cells innervating the muscles of the eyes, face, and mouth. Sensory cells grow shortly after motor cells, projecting their input to the dorsal of the central nervous system. In the forty weeks of gestation, a human brain grows to a two-thirds-size likeness of the adult brain. Its anatomy at birth is remarkably complete. All the typically human cortical areas and nuclear masses of the brainstem are there, containing millions and millions of nerve cells in total. But this general impression is misleading in one important respect. The formation of intercellular

---

[8] The following is an extract from the book *The Oxford Companion to the Mind* edited by Richard L. Gregory on the formation of human brain.

connections, which take up a little extra space but upon which the function of the brain depends, is far from complete. This is, in fact, a huge postnatal manufacture of fine branches where nerve cells seek to form effective contacts with dendrites of other cells. The number of contact points in the cerebral cortex increases astronomically. Each mature cortical cell is estimated to have on average about 10,000 synapses, the greater part of which develops a few months after birth. The total number of synapses in the cortex of one person is about 200,000 times the population of humans on earth."

Eighty-five percent of our neuronal cell bodies are concentrated in the outer part of the hemisphere, this we refer to as our grey matter. Anatomical images show the external view of the brain. The **Cortex** or the outer part of the hemispheres contains neuronal cell bodies that are arranged in six layers. This is where they interpret sensations, initiate movements and performs all the processes involved in thinking, speaking, writing, singing, calculating, creating planning and organizing.

Cerebellum is the second largest part of the brain. It is divided into two tightly folded halves and is responsible for coordinating muscle movements, maintaining balance and helping in some learning processes.

Brainstem connects the brain to the spinal cord. It regulates automatic activities that are vital for survival, such as breathing, heart rate, blood pressure, sleeping and walking, as well as reflex actions such a swallowing and vomiting.

Cerebral hemisphere – each cerebral hemisphere is divided into four lobes. Each lobe is divided into different regions that have their own important functions.

Frontal lobes are the largest of the four lobes of the brain, and are involved in speech, thought, emotions, skilled activities, judgement and social behaviour. This is where our personality lies.

Parietal lobes are where touch and pain are perceived. They deal with information relating to the body's position (proprioception) and interpret taste sensations.

The Temporal lobes are involved in the interpretation and recognition of sounds.

Occipital lobes are the smallest of the four lobes, and are involved in the interpretation and formation of visual images and colour recognition. They are also involved in hearing.

Brain function – The word **intelligence** means "understanding". It refers to the mental ability to reason, plan, solve problems, weigh up options, predict outcomes and think in abstract terms about complex conceptions, such as time and future. It also involves the use of language and the ability to learn quickly and from experience. These higher functions all occur within the brain, and appear to relate to individual anatomical structure such as dendrite branching and cortical convolutions. The dendrites on a neuron cell body divide to form six and sometimes seven or eight successive layers, or orders of branching. These branches are an important determinant of intelligence. The first, second and third level of branching are determined by our genes. The fourth to eighth higher order of branching are partly determined by genes and partly by the level of stimulation and interaction experience during life including within the womb. The more of the higher order branchings that someone has, the more intelligent they are likely to be. The cerebral cortex is folded into convolutions called gyri. Intelligence is also linked with the degree of cortical folding occurring in certain regions, especially within the temporal, occipital lobe in an area called posterior cingulate gyrus.

"Prophet Mohammed (pbuh) reported, the angels asked God; O God, hast Thou created anything greater that thy Throne? He said; yes intellect. They asked; how great is it? He said; alas, your intellect cannot grasp it. Can you count the number of grains of sands? They said; No. God said; I have created intellect in different minds as many as the numbers of grains of sands. Some men have been given one grain, some two, some three, some four some over 100, some 200 and some even more."

Memory – The basic function underpinning intelligence is that of memory, without which every new experience and item of information would have to processed as if were totally unique. Memory is the ability to store, retain and subsequently retrieve information. It allows us to reason by analogy, learning how to solve new problems is a desired outcome. Memory is a wonderful faculty without which we are unable to make the right decision.

It is still poorly understood, many different areas of the brain, such as the hippocampus, amygdala and mammillary bodies are thought to be involved, such as working short term memory, long term memory, spatial memory and emotional memory.

Learning which action to perform must depend upon a system that allows information about the past results to alter the probabilities of the use of the pathways in the future. It is believed that this is done by initially reducing the effectiveness of the wrong pathway then increasing the right one. Perhaps by new synaptic growth. Many special features are required to make such a system effective, and it is not surprising that neuroscientists have not fully unravelled the secret of memory mechanism.

Emotions, human beings experience a number of different emotions, including anger, fear, sadness, disgust, surprise, curiosity, acceptance and joy. There is also confusion, envy, excitement, guilt, compassion, anxiety, grief, embarrassment, caution, loneliness, jealousy, shyness, pleasure, love and lust and among others. Emotions appear to result from the interaction of bodily and mental responses. Many different parts of the brain are involved in the processing of emotions, especially the hypothalamus and the structures within the limbic systems, such as the amygdala and hippocampus, is involved with learning, recognition and new experiences and memory – especially of physical, three dimensional relationships. The limbic system is also closely linked to the detection of smell within the olfactory, which is why some odours trigger strong memories and emotions. Our limbic system develops to regulate the fight or flight stress response, and influences our endocrine system and autonomic nervous system.

After birth, brain development depends on how patterns of stimulation from the outside world meet the varying inner states of brain activity. A stimulus to the infant regulated by the infant's movements and by the behaviour of a caretaker who mediates between the environment and the infant, and the immature brain has powerful control of his caretaker's behaviour especially through emotional expression.

Our brain has got to be without any doubt or any scientific reservation the most ingenious organism designed by its creator. Which man will continue to try to understand and unravel its secrets, its functions and its unique powers? The human brain and how it functions in connection to our spirit, will always remain a mystery to us. In a conscious state, most of us only use a small part of our brain in everyday living and working. When we are asleep, our brain begins to perform in an unconscious state to aid and facilitate our body's requirements. Sometimes we perform on autopilot and make the very best decisions. Medication may not ever be able to fully cure some of the brain diseases. Science will continue in its quest to understand and treat mental illness. A human being can only be considered completely healthy if he has a healthy mind, healthy body and healthy soul.

Perception of Senses

In this section some information is provided on the biological working of our five main senses, smell, taste, sight, touch, hearing, providing extraordinary details. It is fascinating how human senses work with the human anatomy that makes us so unique in the universe. The scientists understanding on working of these senses is truly remarkable and their explanations are breathtaking. These five wonders are worthy of celebration with every human breath.

The reason we start with these sense perceptions is that it's the source of all our knowledge about reality. It is our link to the real world. It's what keeps us true to our personal experiences of our inner world, through our senses we respond with our emotions and actions. These senses are our natural instincts that support our sense of awareness/alertness, that send signals to our mind to start the process of, thinking, focusing, reasoning and responding. Our senses provide very important information for our survival they form a part of our natural qualities they are traits of our personality.

All our senses assist us to learn and gain knowledge to live and survive. We may think of these as inner senses. There are millions of living organisms on this planet; each living species is so wonderfully equipped with the correct balance of sense perceptions to live to provide for itself, to reproduce and survive in its own environment. Their natural measure of sense perception is so perfectly arranged and balanced according to their needs. We can only imagine the chaos it would bring to our life, if human sense of smell and hearing was as good as animals. For example, the polar bears' smelling receptors can smell blood as far as three miles away. The elephants can hear the sound of thunder and lightning as far as 500 km. Humans can only hear the sound of thunder and lightning as far as 25km and so on. If our receptors for - smelling were super sensitive and hearing was ultrasonic, life would be intolerable. Man's infinite and extreme limits of (sight and hearing) are not formed by the evolutionary process but by unique design to suit man's special needs. Every living species is uniquely designed to live and survive on this perfectly equipped planet and all is for the benefit of Man.

And verily, in cattle there is a lesson for you. We give you to drink of that which is in their bellies from between excretions and blood pure milk; palatable to the drinkers.[9]

And from the fruits of date palms and grapes, you derive strong drink and a goodly provision. Verily therein is indeed a sign for people who have wisdom.[10]

And your lord inspired the bee saying, "Take you habitations in the mountains and in tree and in what they erect[11]

Then eat of all fruits and follow the ways of your lord made easy (for you) "there comes forth from their bellies, a drink of varying colour wherein is healing for men. Verily, in this is indeed a sign for people who think[12].

Truly in these divine simple words lay a great hidden wisdom and guidance for mankind to marvel at the unique creation of the honey bees. For man to appreciate their highly sophisticated senses and coordinated teamwork made up of a group – queen bees, drone bees, and worker bees all are devoted to a single purpose- to work and assist to produce a

---

[9] Quran (16:66)
[10] Quran (16:67)
[11] Quran(16:68)
[12] Quran (16:69)

natural wonder of making honey for medicinal/healing purposes. Honey has also been used for centuries as one of nature's natural sweeteners. God inspired the bees to collect nectar and pollen from flowers and fruits. The bee is a marvellous flying machine, a bee can carry a payload of nectar or pollen close to her own weight, even the most advanced aircraft can only take off with a payload of only one quarter its own weight. It truly is a wonder and a miracle that the honeybee can remain airborne with such a load.

Throughout her short life cycle(of only few weeks) the worker bee will work tirelessly collecting pollen, bringing to the hive, cleaning herself, then setting out for more pollen. It takes 300 bees about three weeks to gather 450g of honey. On average, a hive can contain up to 40,000 bees. The scout bees have the task of finding new nectar sources and head out to check all nearby vegetation. If they find nectar, they return to the hive and pass on the exact location with a remarkably intricate dance routine. The scout bee dances in a circle swiftly vibrating her wings, indicating to the worker bee the precise position of the nectar. If the source is further away the dance will be a wagtail roughly in a figure eight with straight centre section. The direction in which she runs the centre and the speed of her movements tell how far to fly in which direction. The bees can be extremely intelligent. Not only do they learn how to overcome obstacles by doing, they can actually learn by watching other bee as well. Bees are also brilliant mathematicians. Bees perform a waggle dance which utilizes speed and directionality to communicate the location of resources relative to their current positon and the sun. Over the years they mastered the art of storing the most amount of honey while using the least amount of resources. The secret behind this efficient honeycomb is due to its hexagonal shape. It is the most volumetrically efficient shape for a two dimensional cellular structure. In other words, if you want to hold a given amount of honey using the minimum amount of wax you make hexagons to store larvae that make the honey. The researchers of bees and the beehive keepers report, nowhere in the world (except man) is there anything to compare with the incredible efficiency of the industry of the honeybees. Inside the beehive, each bee has a special job to do, and the whole process runs smoothly. The Queen bee is the centre of the hive. She accompanies every swarm that you see. The Queen bee is also the largest, her body is specially formed for egg laying so that the eggs can be placed a little above the centre of the cell in the honeycomb. Before depositing her eggs, she inspects each cell to be sure it is properly cleaned by the worker bees. Most bees gather only pollen or nectar. As a bee sucks the nectar from the flower it is stored in her special stomach, ready to transfer to the honey making bees in the hive. Nectar is passed mouth-to-mouth from bee to bee until its moisture content is reduced from about 70% to 20%. Sometimes the nectar is stored at once in the cell in the honeycomb before the mouth-to - mouth working, because some evaporation is caused by the 32.5C temperature inside the hive.

Bees swallow, digest and regurgitate nectar to make honey; this nectar can contain almost 600 compounds. There are at least 40 types of honey; each one has distinctive taste and unique properties. Darker honey tends to have higher antioxidant levels. Most popular are alfalfa, blueberry, buckwheat, clover, manuka, orange blossom, and wildflower.

Honey prevents cancer and heart disease, it contains flavonoids, and antioxidants which help reduce the risk of some types of cancer and heart disease and reduce ulcers and other gastrointestinal disorders.

Recent research shows that honey treatment may help disorders such as ulcers and bacterial gastroenteritis.

All honey is antibacterial because the bees add an enzyme that makes hydrogen peroxide.

Honey is superior in maintaining glycogen levels and improving recovery time to those other sweeteners.

Honey also reduces cough and throat irritation, in a study of 110 children a single dose of buckwheat was just as effective as a single dose of dextromethorphan in relieving nocturnal cough and allowing proper sleep.

Honey has been used in India for at least 400 years and is considered to affect all three of the body's primitive material imbalances positively. It has been useful in improving eyesight, weight loss, curing impotence, bronchial asthma, diarrhoea and nausea.

Some honeys have a low hypoglycaemic index so they don't jolt your blood sugar it helps blood sugar regulation.

External application of honey has been shown to be as effective as conventional treatment with silver sulfadiazine, which helps heal wounds and burns.

Some varieties of honey possess large amounts of friendly bacteria. This includes up to six species of lactobacilli and four species of bifid bacteril, which may explain many of the mysterious therapeutic properties of honey.

Honey antibacterial qualities are particularly useful for the skin and when used with other ingredients, can be used for moisturizing and nourishing.

Our creator with his infinite knowledge said

"God created every moving thing from water; one crawls on its belly, one walks on two legs, another moves on four, God created whatsoever he will, Indeed God has power over everything"[13]

It is our common belief that there are five senses. The ancient philosophers called human senses windows to the soul, and Aristotle enumerated at least five senses sight, hearing, smell, taste, and touch. His influence has been so enduring that many people still speak of the five senses as if there were no other. Yet human skin is also regarded to have sense perception such as hot, cold, pressure and pain. Also sense organs in the muscles, tendons and joints sense balance, equilibrium, gravity, acceleration, and the receptors in the circulatory system are sensitive to carbon dioxide gas in the blood and changes in the blood pressure. There are receptors in the digestive system that appear to mediate such feelings as experience of hunger and thirst.

Smell: our sense of smell, also known as olfaction is provided by chemoreceptors in paired olfactory organs in the nasal cavity on either side of the nasal septum. Chemoreceptor cells that sample odour molecules trigger nerve signals to the brain via the olfactory bulbs situated beneath the frontal cortex on each side. Messages are then

---

[13] Quran (24:45)

relayed to the olfactory cortex of the brain, in the limbic system where smells are interpreted. Different combinations of electrical activity enable us to detect between 4,000 and 10,000 different smells, although we have only 1,000 different olfactory receptor types. Every day we breathe over 23,000 times, bringing in different aromas towards the smell receptors at the top of the nose. Unlike the receptors involved in other senses, smell receptors are directly connected to the brain. Messages are passed to the limbic system, which is involved in the learning, memories and emotions. Smell therefore evokes powerful emotional responses. Our sense of smell was strong at birth – a three-day-old baby can recognize the smell of its own mother's milk. By the age of twenty, our sense of smell is only 82 percent as good as when we were born. By the age of sixty, it is has fallen to 38 percent and by the age of eighty, it is only 28 percent as sensitive as it was at birth.

Consider the two main senses, sight and hearing. Perfect eyesight enables a person to see a star billions of miles away, only a perfect hearing ability would enable the mother to attend a crying infant in the distance.

Sight and hearing are the two most important senses, without these our normal, everyday life would be full of, complications and difficulties which can impose limitations on our mobility and lead to constant dependency and disability.

Only when we look at the structures involved in the formation and arrangement of these senses we are left amazed. Scientific findings now help us to understand the complex working of our senses. It leaves us fascinated with their, complexity, power and range. We are left to wonder how it could all be from a drop of sperm.

The following scientific findings and searched information will help us to have a better understanding of our eyes and vision.

Our **Eyes** can discriminate between more than 100,000 colours, each of which comes in 150 different hues, meaning we can distinguish as many as 10 million different shades. The brightest and darkest light signal our eyes can sense are a factor of one thousand million apart, our vision becomes a million times more sensitive as any brightness dims.

The structures involved in visual perception together form the largest system in the brain. Many of the images we perceive are dependent on the brain interpreting and making assumptions based on prior experience. Neurons within the visual cortex mature at different rates; a new-born baby initially perceives only simply black and white shapes and angles, and then becomes able to recognize more complex patterns and colours such as faces.

Although we have around 126 million rods and cones, only 1.2 million axons pass from our retina to our brain. Each axon therefore carries information processed from around 100 different light-receptor cells

How does it all come together? Consider this scientific explanation on how the human eyes works. The human eye responds to specific stimulus and responds to the amount of light entering the eye. The human eye is remarkable, it accommodates to changing lighting conditions and focuses light rays orientating from various distances for the eye when all components' iris, pupil, lens, macula, optic disc, retina, sclera vitreous) of the eye function properly, light is converted to impulse and conveyed to the brain where an image is perceived.

All the sense organs register a change and transmit the information to the brain.

The function of the inner ear contains parts that are sensitive to acceleration spaces rotations and orientation in the gravitational field. The act of turning round and round, causing swirling movements in the endolymph system inside the ampulla, in the opposite direction of rotation. This deforms the cupula, bending the hair cells which send messages to the cerebellum in the brain, where they are interpreted as rotational motion. In general, the ear consists of three major sections; the outer, middle and inner ear. Sound is collected by the outer ear and funnelled down the middle ear. The sound vibrations cause movement of the eardrum and a chain of three bones connected to the middle ear system server to intensify the energy of the sound vibration and deliver them to the inner ear. Inside the inner ears (cochlea) are thousands of tiny hair-like cells that connect to fibres of the hearing acoustic nerve. Sound vibrations entering the cochlea cause a wave to travel through the fluid filled organ of hearing. This wave causes movement to the hair cells, which then generate electro-chemical signals which travel through the acoustic nerve to the brain where they recognize sounds.

The cochlea in the inner ear is shaped like the shell of a snail and contains the sensory organ of hearing. It is encased in the temporal bone, the hardest bone in the skull. The anatomy of the cochlea is very complex and the function of this wonderful organ is still not completely understood. Our creator states in the holy Quran:

"Was there not a time in the life of man when he was not even a mentionable thing?

Verily we created man from a sperm yoked (to the ovum) to bring out his real substance, then gave him hearing and sight"[14]

---

[14] Quran(76:1&2)

Consciousness

A metaphor that is increasingly used within cognitive psychology to understand the role of consciousness, is that of a theatre (e.g. *Barrs* 1997). According to this metaphor, the brain can be compared to a big theatre where many processes are needed in the background for the play to take place (preparation of the decor, costumes, new players ready to come on stage etc.). These processes work to a large extent independently but they need to be informed about what is going on in the play, in order to synchronise their activities with those of the central event. This is the role of consciousness: making information available to the global workspace so that the activities of the automatic processes can be tuned to one another. The French neuroscientist, Dehaene, presented brain-imaging evidence for the global workspace model (2001) he measured brain activity with FMRI scans. These scans show a very noticeable difference in the brain activity. His test and findings, support the following three observations.

Firstly, most of our information processing takes place automatically without consciousness. Secondly, our attention processes enhance and integrate part of ongoing information processing, and bring it into consciousness. Thirdly, our consciousness awareness is required for operations involved in controlled processing based on knowledge, planning and evaluation.

Among the more perplexing problems of human nature is this: how is it possible that a decent, kindly person may, in short time, find he is killing others with ease? How is such transformation possible? The answer would seem to lie in the understanding of the psychology of obedience. A person who obeys authority does not see himself as responsible for his own actions but rather as an agent executing the wishes of another person or authority. Which in itself can be the subject of controversy? For the psychologist, obedience is neither a good nor evil, but a neutral mechanism whose moral and adaptive aspects depend on the circumstance in which it occurs. A failure to obey law and order to satisfy selfish interest is the hallmark of criminality. Human society as we know it could not exist unless capacities for obedience were present in its members, to respect the society's laws. The role of conscious awareness is to make the information available and the role of conscience is to provide a moral sense of right and wrong the motivation deriving logically from ethical or moral principles that govern a person's thoughts and actions. Consider an educated individual in a modern society, who carries out an act of incest, did he have a conscience, consider a father who rapes his adopted daughter, did he have conscience, a mother who poisoned her autistic son, did she have conscience? When an action is morally wicked or even virtuous, and one finds no pleasure in either, such an individual has no feelings, such a person is considered to have no conscience.

Conscience

Our conscience is formed directly by our cognitive learnings, knowledge and experience.

Before any action is taken, often our 'self' claims to have checked with the natural, inborn conscience (our moral compass) when we choose right from wrong. All of our decisions are based on our moral values, which are guided by our knowledge. The conscience bears witness even to the blind, and the Self cannot escape from this inward judge.

The true bearer of conscience is never free from this internal judicial eye. To the conscious and fearful mind, a right decision can bring enormous joy and happiness from within, and a wrong decision will rebuke the individual with mental suffering and a prolonged torture.

Conscience is a silent voice from within, it guides us voluntarily because it is inborn, a natural intuitive human experience. All of our actions are driven by our desires and personal beliefs. Our instincts are a useful tool and to prevent instincts from running riot, we are given reason too. When reason fails, conviction steps in to guide and provide unfailing strength, this all takes place in the human mind, which is the centre of all out thoughts. Man is able to acquire knowledge of good and evil, man's instincts needs to be teamed with true education and moral training of a faith and firm conviction. First he must realise the importance of a conscience, then to educate and develop it to become a sincere conscience. Our creator has provided us with perfect examples of a man with a conscience to be followed, his prophets also sent divine revelations to be obeyed, which provides man with the true knowledge and rules to obey and live by peacefully with all other God's creations. The divine revelations can save man from losing the balance of mind over body. Man's body and soul have to pull together; both of these entities have to grow in strength, and the two also have to co-operate harmoniously to strengthen the individual conscience and develop the personality. These two separate entities are created in a manner that the one needs the other. The divine nature of man's soul demands complete mastery over the body, in other words the spark of divinity can help a man to achieve the upper hand enabling him to become nearest to God and with God's help, it can be possible to look upon the world with discerning and penetrating eye. That eye can/will see things which otherwise remain hidden.

Even the uneducated Aborigines do not need to learn science or philosophy to know what is wrong and right or to be honest and wise it is in every free man's reach to act justly, to seek counsel from his conscience. When his conscience speaks, his inherent goodness comes forth with the truth, that is virtue expressed. The best audience of virtue is our own conscience.

The best divine gift to humans is their good manners.

The prophet Mohammed stated *"Verily God has distributed among you your dispositions like as He has distributed among you your provisions; verily God gives the world to whom he loves and to whom He love not, but He gives not conscience (to any) except to whom He Loves and whom He gives conscience, He loves him."*

Our conscience is based on the knowledge we have.

Heart

Our heart beats on average seventy times per minute, which is 100,800 times per day, 36,792,000 times per year and over two billion time in an average lifespan. There are around 62,000 miles of blood vessels in our body. The circulation contains around five litres of blood. The slowest blood flow in our body is through the capillaries. The capillaries have a diameter that is just a 30th of human hair. Our capillaries form a network that laid end to end would measure 60,000 miles. The human heart is an amazing organ that functions continually, pumping blood in our body to keep it alive. It would take a dedicated heart specialist to fully understand the cardiovascular system and appreciate how the systemic circulation pumps fresh oxygenated blood from the left side of the heart out to the body to be pumped through arteries to the tissues. Veins carry deoxygenated blood back to the right side of the heart from where it is pumped to the lungs. Each heartbeat consists of three phases resting, atrial contraction, and then ventricular contraction. It truly is an ingenious design.

Modern sciences have made biological studies of its functions and have found ways to improve blood quality and manipulate blood circulation, and also have introduced the common use of the pacemaker to control and regulate the human heartbeat.

Over the centuries, especially in the last fifty years, medical experts have made enormous progress to understand the interconnecting functions and interactions of the heart with the rest of the body that it keeps alive. In the modern world, the scientists continue in their quest to discover new kinds of medical treatments and cures for the human heart. The surgical pioneers are now able to perform operations once considered impossible. The new microsurgery surgery operations have made so many impossible tasks now possible.

Still heart failure is the biggest cause of human death.

Human psychology is the scientific study of the human mind and its functions. Anatomy is the scientific study of bodily structures and their functions.

Our heart is the engine that makes the other organs function.

When we begin to describe our feelings, we relate them to our heart and consider it to be the seat of all our emotions, such as love, hate, envy, jealousy, happiness, sorrow.

Our heart is at the very core of our feelings that inspires all our actions.

In some cases, the heart-felt response becomes the very cause of the heart's own failure.

There are thirty-one pairs of nerves that emerge from the spinal cord to different parts of the body. Sensory fibres extend from the rear of our spinal cord (dorsal) to join motor fibres (ventral) from the front. The spinal nerves relay sensory information form the body to the brain, and send back motor instructions relating to voluntary and involuntary actions. Survival sometimes requires an instant response, so certain automatic reflex actions occur at the level of the spinal nerves. In this instance, a sensory neuron connects with a motor neuron via a short interneuron to produce a reflex arc. For an example, when you instantly withdraw your finger form a flame, a reflex arc is involved, your finger moves milliseconds before the pain signal travels up the spinal cord to reach your brain.

Our heartfelt emotions strongly energise our nervous system, in fact, our brain is the organ of thought, and its sensory processing serves many aspects, i.e. to respond, act and communicate. Our sense perceptions transmit signals to our brain where our wonderful faculty of memory plays its part to set our emotions in play, which are expressed by our physical organs.

Broadly stating, it is our brain that contains all the knowledge and information which our memories transmit to our inherent senses that give rise to our emotions and our actions. The decision may have been reached by our heart, which it intuitively forms, from its past experience which is served and commissioned by our memories. The course of action we take would be by our personal choice which is executed with our free will. This free will is our divine gift it is entirely up to us to choose, love over hate compassion over revenge or even forgiveness. We simply act and decide on the basis of our own experiences.

Our personal experience with other humans also contributes to our choices. If we have not experienced personal care, compassion and love from our parents and guardians, can we love?

If we have not experienced forgiveness or mercy, can we be compassionate and merciful?

Birds, fish, and all animals show love care and compassion to their offspring, they toil every hardship of nature to provide food and care for their offspring, who survived in the natural world because they learnt and remember how it was provided to them.

There are millions of different species on this planet earth; we humans are the greatest of all God's creations. Sometimes we are simply led by our feelings, emotions, overwhelming desires and passions. Logic and reason leads us to make a free choice for the satisfaction of some of our physical needs, some for our mental satisfaction, this we pursue with our inborn determination and zeal. Sometimes an obsessed person may spend a whole lifetime working to realise a personal dream to fulfil his ambition for personal satisfaction.

The ultimate prize we seek is the contentment and satisfaction of our heart.

Generally speaking, when we do finally achieve our ultimate goal, our personal dream, having made so many personal sacrifices in pursuit of it, sometimes only the bearer knows the final satisfaction achieved is not as he/she originally perceived. It seldom is. Human ambition is not satisfied even on the summits of glory. The worldly achievements fail to bring a permanent contentment to a heart. If we are sincere to ourselves and delve into the depth of our heart, we may realise that at the very peak moment of gaining our achievements, our heart can suddenly begin to feel uncomfortable and restless, unable to explain with good reason, despite gaining the prize we are not fully content, because our heart is in need of something else. It still feels something is missing it remains unfulfilled and is still in search of more. Sometimes we may experience and feel a certain kind of emptiness. A sincere person deep down only to his inner self would confess he is not fully content. He remains in search of more, the longing quest for the final satisfaction of enduring peace, can still remain far in the distance and still remain elusive. Sometimes, sudden impulses may give rise to a certain kind of notion from the heart. One can be tempted to satisfy his/her immediate physical needs, sometimes sudden, harsh, impulsive actions taken without knowledge or deliberation of faith or conviction. Then this self is likely to be tempted on impulse and passion alone, only for temporary satisfactions of the heart. In these moments, you may well ask yourself, was I guided by conviction or conscience, was the choice from my heart? Did I exercise free will, simply to gain temporary satisfaction and contentment for the heart? Before one resorts to finding a temporary escape by resorting to use of alcohol, drugs, or other self-harming addictions, which only leads to a path of self-destruction?

One must examine the course of one's action at the outset and consider its final outcome. His/her addictions will have its effect on his health, work and family. Such addiction may bring a brief, temporary escape, comfort, or satisfaction. Eventually in time the solution, the addiction will become the main problem itself.

Our creator and maker of our heart reminds us he placed one heart in our body, he is fully aware of what it experiences at every moment of our life. *"He knows what is in the heavens and on earth and He knows what you conceal and what you reveal. And Allah is the All-knower of what is in the breasts of men."* Quran 24:4. God, the maker of our heart states, the true contentment of our heart lies with God, in God's remembrance.

When you remember God, God remembers you, when you forget God, God forgets you.

When you do remember God, with the correct knowledge, faith, conviction and practice, the true experience of our heart can be achieved. This is because the "heart" is a kind of inner intuition or insight which, in the beautiful words of Poet Rumi, "Feeds on the rays of the sun and brings us into contact with aspects of Reality other than open to sense perception."

The heart actually sees if properly interpreted and is never false. It must not be regarded as a mastery or a special faculty it is rather a mode of dealing with reality in which sensation in the physiological senses does not play any part. To describe it as psychic, mystical or supernatural does not distract from its value as an experience. It is real experience, if for a moment we consider a dream in which the experience of the individual is very real in seeing, eating, hearing, and that individual comes to have knowledge of future events that will take place, something which he/she cannot explain with logic and reason or with any physical proof. Which are only his/her perceptions and only his/her account, from his/her memories.

It is this, the real experience which we have to consider for our personal experience and give more importance to. Our life's quest must be to understand our own heart and improve our character with real knowledge, thus lifting the veil from the eyes of the heart so as to see the mysterious relation between man and his maker and to be filled with a sense of awe and reverence in the presence of an omniscient holy being who pervades the universe. This attitude of the mind, this enlightenment, is real knowledge.

When our heart is as clean as a mirror, when it is purified it can behold the images which are out of this world of earth and water, that defy logic and reason.

The prophet Mohammed (pbuh) has also have reported to have stated

"Verily, in the body there is piece of flesh: when it is in good condition, the whole body is in good condition: when it is corrupt, the whole body is corrupt: it is the Heart."

Personality

The origin and study of human physiology dates back to at least 420 B.C. and the time of Hippocrates, the father of medicine. Personal achievement tests in China date back two thousand years. The Chinese Han dynasty (206BCE-220CE) use a standardised personality test to select and promote civil servants in an objective way. In the nineteenth century, Edwin Boring (1886-1968) was the first great historian of psychology. He published and extremely popular book, *A History of Experimental Psychology* (1st edition 1929, 2nd revised edition 1950) in which he introduced the five school as the core of early psychology, and idea that have ever since pervaded psychology textbooks.

In this section, some information is provided on the manifestation of personality. Indicating which lobe of our brain (cortex) we actually use that form some of our personality traits. Some of the genes you inherit determine your visible features, such as your skin, hair and eye colour. The dendrites on a neuron cell body divide to form six and sometimes seven or eight successive layers, or orders of branching. These branchings are an important determinant of intelligence. Since 1980, a large number of personality questionnaires have been developed. The researchers more or less settled on a total five fundamental traits commonly recognised to describe a personality using the acronym

OCEAN. Also Sigmund Freud's analogy of id, ego and superego, the thoughts of philosophers Aristotle, Kent, Hume, Locke and Saint Augustin and the prophet Mohammed, their contributions help us to understand the very formation and structure of our personality. The important role of parents in raising their child, the influence of society and culture, all these factors contribute in making a personality. In this section, the importance of education, knowledge and faith in self and God is observed, an integral part of any personality.

Cutting-edge anatomical images of the brain show that the frontal lobes are the largest of the four lobes of the brain, and are involved in speech, thought, emotions, skills activities, judgement and social behaviour. This is where your personality lies. These higher functions all occur within our brain, and they appear to relate to individual anatomical structures such as dendrite branching and cortical convolutions. The dendrites on neurones divide to form six and sometimes seven or eight successive layers or orders of branching. These branching are an important determinant of intelligence. The first, second, and the third levels of branching are determined by our genes. The fourth to eighth higher orders of branching are partly determined by our genes and partly by the level of stimulation and interaction experience during early life – including in the womb. The more of the higher-order branching that someone has the more intelligent they are likely to be.

Some physiologists hold the view that the hormones secreted by endocrine glands play a decisive role in the growth and the normal functioning of personality.

The word personality stems from the Latin word persona meaning the mask – the Greek thespians used to wear a mask to perform as a character in a play which represented the aspect of his personality to the audience.

The search for personality traits started when the American psychologist Gordon Allport in the 1930s tried to discover the structure that underlies the adjectives people use to describe each other. In the 1980s physiatrists explored using many different questionnaires to measure and test different personalities. The researchers more or less settled on a total of five fundamental traits. A large number of personality questionnaires have been developed using the acronym OCEAN. Openness (your ability to keep an open mind) Conscientiousness (your tendency to be careful in your decision-making process) Extroversion (your tendency to be and outgoing person) Agreeableness (your tendency to get along with others, in social situations) and Neuroticism (your tendency to portray negative emotions, such as anxiety or anger). These five traits are used in personality tests, and are also used to help in screening job applicants, can be used for clinical evaluation of psychological issues, and can be used repetitively to judge the effectiveness or ineffectiveness of psychological therapy.

The study of personality is based on observation or experience rather than theory or logic. Theories of human personalities have been many since humans speculated about why they act as they do. The term personality has been given many meanings but the core has been the traits or the characteristics within an individual. The emphasis has been in two aspects, first the individual's characteristics which are common with others and secondly his more distinguished characteristics in comparison to others. It is this unique combination of the two aspects in an individual that have manifested and transformed the individual's personality as to how they are described by someone else who has come to know them.

In psychology, personality is studied in the three main areas. First to construct a coherent picture of a person as to how he or she behaves in major psychological processes, the second area is the individual difference or how people differ from one another. The third area is the emphasis on examining human nature, how people are similar to one another's viewpoint, merge together in the study of personality The social physiologists tend to attach greater importance to the social milieu in which the human child grows up. Personality emerges through the process of socialization.

The famous psychoanalyst **Sigmund Freud**[15] divides human personality into three significant components;

"The ego, super ego, and id, the id acts according to the pleasure principle, demanding immediate gratification of its

---

[15] Sigmund Freud was an Austrian neurologist and the founder of psychoanalysis, a clinical method for treating psychopathology through dialogue between a patient and a psychoanalyst.
Born: May 6, 1856, Příbor, Czech Republic
Died: September 23, 1939, Hampstead

need regardless of external environment, the ego then must emerge in order to realistically meet the wishes and demands of the id in accordance with the outside world, adhering to reality principle. Finally, the superego inculcates moral judgment and societal rules upon the ego, thus forcing the demands of the id to meet not only realistically but morally. The superego is the last function of the personality to develop, and is the embodiment of parental/social ideals established during childhood. According to Freud, personality is based on the dynamic interactions of these three components. He formulated the idea that in every individual there is a coherent organization of mental processes, which we call his ego. This ego includes consciousness, and it controls the approaches to motility, i.e. to discharge of excitation to the external world, it is this institution in the mind which regulates its own entire constituent processes which goes to sleep at night. The ego is the mediator between the id and the super-ego trying to ensure that the needs of the id and the superego are satisfied. It is said, to operate on a reality principle, meaning it deals with the id and superego; allowing them to express their desires, drives and morals in realistic and socially appropriate ways. It is said that the ego stands for reason and caution, developing with age. Sigmund Freud had used an analogy which likened to a rider and a horse; the ego being the rider while the id being the horse. The horse provides the energy and the means of obtaining the energy and the information needed, while the rider ultimately controls the direction it wants to go. However, due to unfavourable conditions, sometimes the horse makes its own decisions over the rocky terrain. When the ego is personified, it is like a slave to three harsh masters; the id, the superego and the external world. It has to do its best to suit all three, thus constantly feeling hemmed in by the danger of causing discontent on the two other sides. It is said, however, that the ego seems to be more loyal to the id, preferring to gloss over the finer details of reality to minimize conflicts while pretending to have regard for reality.

But the super ego seems to be constantly inferior. To overcome this, ego employs defence mechanisms. The defence mechanisms are not done so directly or consciously.

They lessen the tension by covering up our impulses that are threatening.

"Philosopher **Aristotle's**[16] thoughts on personality describe the analytic process by which we divide kinds of beings to establish an essence He works gradually from the broadest down to narrower classifications. Aristotle points out that knowledge is valuable, however knowledge of the soul is even more so, "for the soul is... the first principle of living things." "Philosopher **Kant's**[17] thoughts on personality-

---

[16]Aristotle was a Greek philosopher and scientist born in the city of Stagira, Chalkidice, on the northern periphery of Classical Greece. His father, Nicomachus, died when Aristotle was a child, where after Pyroxenes of Atreus became his guardian.
Born: 384 BC, Stagira, Aristotelis, Greece
Died: 322 BC, Chalcis, Greece

[17] German philosopher Immanuel **Kant** devised an **argument** from **morality** based on practical reason. **Kant argued** that the goal of humanity is to achieve

starts by saying that we can experience our own states of consciousness, our thoughts, feelings, and desires and so on: and we can attribute them to an "absolute subject". Kant believes that we cannot know, and cannot experience this "absolute subject" instead we should regard it as merely an "idea of reason."

Philosopher **Hume**[18] wrote the following concerning human understanding:

"It is universally acknowledged that there is a great uniformity among the actions of men, in all nations and ages, and that human nature remains still the same, in its principles and operations. The same motives always produce the same actions: The same events follow from the same causes, ambition, avarice, self-love, vanity, friendship, generosity, and public spirit. These passions, mixed in various degrees, and distributed through society, have been from the beginning of the world and still are the source of all the

---

perfect happiness and virtue (the summon bone) and believed that an afterlife must exist in order for this to be possible, and that God must exist to provide this.

[18] Locke FRS was an English philosopher and physician, widely regarded as one of the most influential of Enlightenment thinkers and commonly known as the "Father of Liberalism"
Born: August 29, 1632, Wrington
Died: October 28, 1704, High Laver

actions and enterprises, which have ever been observed among mankind. "

John Locke stated **in** 1689 that personal identity (the self) depends on consciousness and not on substance or on the soul. We are the same person to the extent that we are conscious of our past and future thoughts and actions in the same way as we are conscious of our present thoughts and actions. Lock also argues that you may be judged only for the acts of your body as this is apparent to all but God; however you are in truth only responsible for the acts for you are conscious. This forms the basis of insanity.

Saint Augustine's[19] thoughts on personality. As a Christian, Augustine is committed to the belief that God created the human soul, "God then, made man in his own image. For he created for him a soul endowed with reason and intelligence, so that he might excel all the creatures of the earth, air and sea." Augustine admits that other animals surpass us in strength and other physical abilities, but avers that our superiority consists in our having a rational soul or a mind, which should rule the other dimensions of human nature if we are to be well ordered. "Man, then is a rational soul with a mortal and earthly body in its service."

19

Saint Auguine of Hippo, also known as Saint Augustine, Saint Austin, or Blessed Augustine, was an early Christian theologian and philosopher whose writings influenced the development of Western Christianity and Western philosophy.
Born: November 13, 354 AD, Thagaste
Died: August 28, 430 AD, Hippo Regius, Algeria

This is platonic by nature, focusing on the soul and not the body, but later he describes a more Aristotelian definition, "Man is an animal, rational and mortal."

Augustine believes that the mind or rational soul is independent of the body.

We try to locate the soul in the body by a physical location, but it is in fact not a physical thing but as an aware, animating motivating people.

For centuries, it has been common belief the very first institution that any child naturally learns from is his home, from his parents. Children not only acquire physical resemblances of his parents, also his intelligence. Now, the DNA of a brain supports and confirms these findings. – The brains, the dendrites on a neuron cell body are divided into anywhere from six and sometimes seven or eight successive layers. The first three to four are important to determinant the intelligence, determined by our genes. The fourth to eighth is partly determined by our genes and partly by the level of stimulation and interaction experience of early life including within the womb.

The psychoanalysts who provide us with analytical theories have provided us with the following findings. A child may be living with parents who are affectionate and permissive, affectionate and controlling hostile and permissive and controlling. Some psychiatrists state each different case of the parent tends to produce a different kind of personality of the child.

The parents are responsible for laying the foundation of their child's personality which begins to take its form from infancy.

Locke the philosopher has so eloquently summed up in the following words;

"The power, then, that parents have over their children arises from the duty which is incumbent on them to take care of their offspring during the imperfect state of childhood. To inform the mind, and govern the actions of their yet ignorant none age, until reason shall take its place and ease them of that trouble, is what the children want and the parents are bound to. For God having given man an understanding to direct his action, has allowed him with a freedom of will and liberty of acting, as properly belonging thereunto within the bounds of that law he is under. But whilst he is in an estate wherein he has no understanding of his own to direct his will, he is not to have his own will too follow. He that understands for him must will for him too, he must prescribe to him will and regulate his actions."

The parents provide the stimuli in which the child grows up. The child's parents approach to life will provide many answers towards understanding their child's personality. The parents own fundamental beliefs which contribute towards the very foundation of their own personality, like their faith, beliefs, values, desires and passions all actually provide the structure and form to their child's personality. Their early influence has given shape to the child's personality.

Those who are concerned with the development and understanding of personality must make religious beliefs and faith the integral part of life and it should occupy the central palace in everyone's personality.

The prophet Muhammed was sent by God as guidance for all mankind.

"In the words of the prophet the best gift that a parent can bestow on his child is good character. God states in a holy scripture every child born is not only pure and innocent but a true candidate for a faith, it is his parent that makes him into a Muslim, Christian, Jew ,Hindu or a believer in any other faith or finds himself as an atheist. "

One of the most important decisions that any human takes in this life is to believe in his creator, God, to have faith it is the very foundation of any personality. To believe in a religion indicates the direction for that personality. His religious faith can provide him with the inner peace in this life. A resolute faith finds physical strength, and his strong conviction finds true guidance from within, from the divine spark – his spirit. No one born into this world has a choice of his parents, time, place, or faith. Time, place and culture will have its own influences on the child's personality. As parents, initially we bear all the responsibility for bringing up our child- to provide food, love, care and education. It is built in us, it is a part of our natural instincts. For which we are rewarded with love and joy in seeing our child happy. Such kinds of experiences are unique satisfactions which is incomparable for many fortunate parents.

First, we as parents must ask ourselves, we had a choice either to believe or not in God.

For which we will be held accountable. Every child has a right to ask his parent, did they make the right choice of religious faith. Did they set a good example of good character for their child's personality, did they fulfil their responsibility? It naturally falls upon the parents to try to be a good role model. The first step for the parents is to realise and question their own state of mind regarding their own religious faith. They must pause, and also examine every aspect of their own daily life. It is in most cases as parents we have to pass on to our children our own best experience as our parents did for us. We may have been passive learners and teachers most of the time without questioning any aspects of our way of life.

As mentioned previously our first duty is to our immediate self, our own needs, our desires, our feelings, our beliefs, as we become more independent to fulfil our own needs and our carnal desires, we exercise our right at home and demand it in society. We apply our own house rules and live by societal laws. In today's modern society the divine laws at home at work and in society are constantly ignored, in nearly every aspect of our lives.

In almost every human relationship the mutual respect and trust has evaporated with time, every country has its own legislation which is constantly updated to please the majority of its own voters. Legislators would have us believe no one is above the law, the law too has its limits and is often bound by its own geography. Often these laws encourage us to compromise our faith and our core religious beliefs. Then, the whole of society begins to exercise and enjoy its many popular freedoms of self-gratifications involving all kinds of unnatural sexual activities and take pleasure in all forbidden addictions to intoxicate their bodies. This kind of freedom and liberty produce a promiscuous society, such culture begins to influence and shape many vulnerable personalities. Such a culture may produce popular personalities, but, with serious issues of drinks; drugs, prostitution and human sex slavery, and gambling, these addictions bring serious illness and are always the cause of premature deaths. These are some of the corrosive elements that have destroyed many communities and nations in the past, even now, it has become a very difficult challenge for a parent to help form and nurture a virtuous personality.

In some centuries, every new changes in its laws provides freedom of more and new choices. Some personalities may feel that they have won personal freedom and independence that fulfils their passion and personal desires, it may be perceived as a vital victory for them, in fact in some cases fighting for more freedom has subject them to a narrow vision which only leads their personality to a quick and destructive end. These protesting personalities are weak they have subjected themselves to new laws and rule of human relationship to harmful addictions and have very little control over themselves and their passions. They may have gained new traits which describe their personality. When divine laws and rules of life on earth are ignored because of popular opinions, then the laws of the land fails to act as deterrent, law is unable to punish the criminal adequately, allowing the dark clouds of injustice and inequality to prevail.

In a very short time, this too will become part of our human history, as we found with our forefathers.

Is it possible to predict the behaviour of any personality?

It is very difficult to make any future predictions about any personalities or their sudden change in behaver. Personal belief and ill intention often remain hidden within a personality. Sometimes negative emotions and bad feelings and ill intentions can remain dormant within a personality, which are only known to its bearer, which are not easily noticeable and cannot be detected. Over the centuries, it has always been a part of a potential employers' practice to check and approve the applicant for the vacancy offered. Professional skill and experience does not always reflect the true essences of a personality because a person's beliefs and skills are two separate entities. While the academic achievements can be verified and the skills of the applicant can be tested, the personality tests often carried out via a set of questions are not reliable or definitive and even the accuracy of polygraph test is only 90-95%. The polygraph instrument is a scientific, diagnostic instrument, which is often called the "lie detector "it would be more appropriate, however, to call it the truth verifier. These are only used in higher circles of government, linked and often state funded institutions. Lie detectors are often used after the crime has been committed. Their results are not infallible. It is not possible to detect from appearance the belief and internal motives of a perfectly normal person, or by any scientific, technical means. Only a person of true conscience and faith in God and fear of God alone, is the only potent deterrent which is always present in a believer which can guide and prevent a personality not to commit a crime.

Only a personality which believes in God and fears God, knows and remembers that their every thought, every intention and every action is known to God, from which there is no escape. The true believer in the hereafter also knows, every action of his personality carried out in this worldly life will be accounted for and compensated accordingly in regards to whether it was good or bad. Our creator states:

It is He who created the heavens and the earth in six stages, then assumed the throne. He knows whatsoever enters the earth, and whatsoever comes out of it, and what comes down from the sky and what goes up to it; and he is with you whosesoever you may be, and He perceives whatsoever you do[20]

If the fear of God is not present and the belief in accountability does not exist, the fear of divine punishment does not act as a deterrent. Then any personality is capable of committing the most serious and inhumane crimes. To mention a few, a priest or a imam or a celebrity will abuse a child, a nurse would cause a death, a doctor would abuse patients' trust, a solicitor or an accountant would compromise clients confidentiality, a scientist would be partisan to genocide or a despot ruler may kill his own citizens. These personalities, when they are meant to serve the public's best interest, themselves fall victim to their evil spirits and take human lives or commit the most unimaginable crimes on his fellow man. History bears witness, too many heinous crimes have been committed by the rulers and professionals with public responsibility. Their work ethics, code of conduct, integrity, objectivity, professional behaviour, confidentiality, professional competence and due care, for other human loses all importance, at the time when they are so committed to their own desires and beliefs, without the fear of any consequence commit the crimes. They are either subjected to their greed,

---

[20] Quran(57:4)

lust, eminence, pride anger or revenge/justice which blinds their consciences. To themselves, they are all ways justifying their actions, and take comfort from the thought that they will never face justice. To them only the life of this world matters, their philosophy of life is without faith or fear, they have simply chosen to ignore and disbelieve that there will be accountability of all their actions, after death, from which there is no escape, our creator reminds us, fear death and the day of resurrection.

Then (again) surely, you will be resurrected on the day of Resurrection[21]

Does man (a disbeliever) think that we shall not assemble his bones?[22]

Yes, we are able to put together in perfect order the tips of his fingers[23]

In life, every personality needs to exercise his faith in the creator. For us human beings, our moral compass should be energised from the guidance of divine hope and fear, it should rule our behaviour. Only through its application in life where divine rule and order is obtained and justice prevails.

It is only through hope man is meant to continue – the constant fear of divine accountability keeps him on track, knowing, that, his every action is being monitored and recorded. The two important elements in human life, the presence of hope and fear are like to two wings of any bird, it cannot fly for long without the two in perfect order. Every

---

[21] Quran(23:16)
[22] Quran(75:3)
[23] Quran(75:4)

personality must believe in its accountability, the angels who are constantly monitoring his/her every thought and recording every action taken; only hope and fear can keep us humans on the right course in this worldly life. Only the divine accountability can deliver the correct rewards for our every good intentions and actions. Only true reality (God) can know what we hide what we reveal, and only he knows that true reality is the only hope that is eternal. It has always been there with us from the moment it created us. That is God, supreme being, the supernatural being conceived as the perfect and omnipotent and omniscient originator and ruler of the universe, the object of worship in a monotheistic religion. Only God can hold us accountable.

We shall fix the scales of justice on the day of resurrections, that none will be wronged in the least; and even if it were equal to a mustard seed in weight we shall take it (into account) we are sufficient for computation.[24]

---

[24] Quran(21:47)

Human Nature

When our creator said to the angels

"Verily I am going to place (mankind) generation after generation on earth " They said, "Will you place there in those who will make mischief there in and shed blood- while we glorify you with praise and thanks and sanctify you?" He Allah said I know which you do not know[25]

And he taught Adam all the names of (everything) then he showed them to the Angels and said, "Tell me the names of these if you are truthful[26]

They (angels) said, "Glorified are you, we have no knowledge except what you have taught us. Verily it is you, the knower, the All-wise."[27]

Our creator with his infinite knowledge and wisdom, created all humans equal. He has also stated that, every day spent on this earth will be a test of each personality and character. The best human is he who remains positively committed to this test. God has also reminded us, that, every good or bad deed of every individual is being recorded by the appointed angels– they will produce every individual's record

[25] Quran (2:30)
[26] Quran(2:31)
[27] Quran(2:32)

on judgement day; our creator will decide our reward by placing us in heaven or hell.

To teach and guide humans to achieve this reward, he sent forth prophets to mankind with holy scriptures, a divine guidance for mankind to live by. The prophets lived amongst the humans. They lived as perfect role models for men to follow. Their teachings and practices are all preserved in the holy scriptures. The Quran revealed to his last prophet, Mohammed, the only divine revelation which remains in its original form. To date this still remains unchallenged which provides us with a code of practise – a complete way of life. It is true knowledge a complete guidance for all mankind to live by. Our creator has placed each man as his vice-regent, (his ambassador/administrator) on earth.

As humans we share with animals' internal and external senses. Superiority of man lies in his conscious awareness. Man is also endowed with two further qualities to acquire knowledge and use his free will, these enable him to be self-aware and to make choices. Man is able to use his faculties to acquire and learn knowledge.

His cognitive experiences and knowledge provides him with guidance. His self-awareness provides him with the power to generalise the conceptions of all intellectual truths. His will inspires the desire in him to acquire the objective and to consider all consequences. His actions are guided by his reason based on his knowledge. The capacity for knowledge varies according to the latent power of each man. They are varied stages, a child cannot know the stage that an adult knows, a learned man cannot know what the scholar knows, the scholar does not know to the extent of what a philosopher knows, the philosopher cannot know of the experiences that a saint has, the saint does not have the experience or the knowledge of what a prophet knows. Further stages are possible, for divine knowledge knows no bounds. Pure thoughts are the signpost to direct knowledge (divine inspirations). The highest stages are reached by one to whom all truths and realities are revealed intuitively, who by the virtue of his exalted position enjoys direct communion and close relation with the Most Holy.

As mentioned in one of the sayings of the Prophet Mohammed, (about God)

"The desire of the virtuous is to hold communion with me and I long to look at them, He who approaches me a span I approach him an arm. The divine favours are not withheld it is the quality of the heart its impurities that form the barrier and fails to receive the divine blessing."

The superiority of man consists in being cognisant of divine attributes and actions and there lies his perfection. A man uses his qualities of reason and will. Let him look up reason as his monarch setting on the thrown of his heart, let his imagination be his ambassador, let his memory be his treasurer, let his speech be his interpreter, let his limbs be his clerks, let his senses act as his spies. If all his senses discharge all the duties allocated to them, if every faculty of man does what it was created, then such a service would be a real reason to give thanks to our creator. When man neglects to learn and obtain true knowledge about himself and his creator he fails to understand his true role in life as God's representative. He is liable to lose his way, his sense of direction; negative temptations can be overpowering that might may lead him to wonder off in the wrong direction. The body can easily overpower the sprit within; he is liable to deprive himself of the endless possibilities of divine blessing. He may have also failed to appreciate the true limits of his inner senses. He may have totally ignored to rekindle the divine spark in him, his only direct connection with his creator through his spirit – his soul. The food for the soul is true knowledge, if practiced can ignite the spark to develop his relationship with his creator. Man's weakness lies in not being able to maintain a clear balance between his obligations to his creator and to fulfil and satisfy his own immediate needs. When his own personal desires and passions take a strong hold of him, his role as God's ambassador begins to weaken. There are four elements that contribute towards his weakness and fall. These elements eventually materialise and take form of man's governing behaviour, which can be seen and described as someone who is a beastly, brutish, and satanic or a saintly man.

The seeds of these natural elements are to be found in everyman; they are also being developed and nurtured further by man's own knowledge they take further strength from his own experiences, sometimes these elements are shaped by strong external influences. These elements can sometimes lay dormant but eventually emerge. These can be described as, for example- as of man's behaviour pattern to a pig, a dog, a devil, or a saint. The pig has an appetite which is repulsive, not for its form but for it lust and gluttony. The dogs are his passion which barks and bites others and cause injury. The Devil instigates the former two which dims his light of reason. The saint who is guided by his true learning also receives support from his spirit. He truly values the inner guidance which helps him to maintain control over these elements. The saint does not give in to his passions or ever yield to his personal desires for immediate self-gratification or any material gain. The saint is always vigilant because of his learning and understanding of the divine guidance and he is always seeking refuge in his creator from the seductive traps of evil. The evil is always with him, to manipulate, to sway his thoughts, to trick him to tip the balance of these four elements of man's behaviour, to misguide him towards his ruin. Our creator has forewarned us about the evil, with the following words.

"In the name of Allah the most gracious, the most merciful,

Say; I Seek refuge with (Allah), the lord of mankind.

The king of mankind,

The Allah (God) of mankind,

From the evil of the whisperer (devil who whispers evil in the heart of men)

Who withdraws (From his whispering in one's heart after one remembers Allah?)

Who whispers in the breasts of mankind,[28]

The prophet Mohammad has said, "On the day of resurrection Allah will grasp the whole planet Earth by his hand and all the heavens in his right hand and then will say

---

[28] Quran(114:1-5)

"I am the king where are the kings of the earth, his obligation to himself of seeking the basic needs to sustain his life." (Ref. Sahih Al-Bukhari 9/7412, 7413)

It is fundamental for every man to learn of his obligation towards his creator and maintain balance in life between his obligations to his creator and himself (in seeking his basic needs to sustain life.) When this balance is lost, when greater importance is given to this life which makes him neglect his creator, when (in a man) the inward push of life is always directing him in perusing his own passion and desires beyond his basic needs. Then you have clearly made a conscious decision to pursue the end goal, which is important to you. The splendour, fame and glory of this world are a great temptation for us all. The beauty of this world is alluring and very seductive, it is all a temporarily show for this life. Two desires always remain strong in us, one is to accumulate wealth the other to live a longer life.

The giver of this life reminds us with the following;

Know that the life of this world is only play and amusement, pump and mutual boasting among you, and rivalry in respect of wealth and children. (It is) as the likeness of vegetation after rain, thereof the growth is pleasing to the tiller; afterwards it dries up and you see it turning yellow ; then it became straw, But in the hereafter (there is) a sever torment(for disbelievers- evildoers) and (there is) forgiveness from Allah and (his)Good pleasure (for

believers – good doers) and the life this world is only a deceiving enjoyment.[29]

For self and spirit, the end purpose of all human efforts in life are to achieve satisfaction and contentment. While personal and material benefits are for the physical self in this life. Material benefits provide no contentment to the spirit, unless the achievements have been obtained with the co-operation of the spirit. The divine knowledge's practice provides the essential purity to the spirit to achieve higher aims. This provides greater influence over the physical and material needs of man. Our spirit's contentment is not only unique for this world; it can also be the next life which is eternal. Our divine spirit co-operates and guides only the saintly element of human behaviours. In this world, you may be a king, or an emperor, no award, or accolade, or any conquest of people or land, or even if acquired all the material wealth of this world, will bring- true contentment to the spirit of man unless the spirit's creator wills it.

The physical pleasures of this world are made very attractive and pleasing to lure man, through which his human weakness are explored by the Devil. Our only defence lies in physically practicing our faith, the real fruit of our learning is **fear of God** in our minds and in our actions. If we have ignored our spirit in this life, it will abandon us on the bridge to the next life, when we desperately seek its favourable accountability and references, for eternal happiness and contentment towards the next life. It will not show any

---

[29] Quran (57:20)

sympathy for its lifelong partner – its courier – our body. The Devil has then won by manipulating our mind and body – we have failed our spirit, because we failed to maintain a balance between the needs of our body and spirit, and towards our obligation to our creator.

Faith in Self and Creator

The process of faith in one's own self and self-capabilities begins with conscious awareness, using sense perceptions, experiences and memories. I realising I am alive, in good health and free from any pressure distractions. I enjoy the freedom of my own choices. The choice made for my personal safety is without any obligation, influence or due to any enticements. I feel completely in control and confident of my own decision. When the self is faced with the risk of any physical danger, its inborn qualities and instincts are always guiding it, self always makes the right decision for its own safety which is paramount and natural. Sometimes we take a chance and take part in risks and dangerous activities with confidence, it is only because we have learned to take control of the possible risks involved. During these risky moments, our memories remind and assure us to have self-confidence which we have built through our learning experiences. These repetitive exercises increase our confidence with each progressive attempt. Our belief in our ability is firm, now we have greater faith in our self. Some tasks before, which were full of perils and inherent dangers are now undertaken continuously with faith and great confidence. Most of these tasks are taken consciously because our memories serve as a polite reminder and give us inner encouragement to make the next attempt. In some cases, a determined enthusiast seeks a personal perfection for a higher aim and distinction, even to compete for a prize. Now this experienced self feels completely in control when running down the stairs, using a knife, electrical appliances, garden tools, driving a car, riding a motorbike, a speed boat or riding a horse, sky diving, even bungee jumping. In time, with much experience and skill, a mature self begins to gloat over its own physical capabilities and control, now it can perform many tasks simultaneously. This is the result of cognitive experience, achieved with one's own intellect and wisdom. The learning experience has assured the self to have faith in one's self and trust his own competence. If this self is a passenger in a bus, a train, an aeroplane, in a ship or hot air balloon, or a space rocket, the individual would have little or no control over the means of its travel. Now as a passenger, he has to put his or her trust in the machines, also have confidence in the competence of its operators. At the first sign of danger, our body's sympathetic nervous system initiates the 'fight or flight' response by triggering the release of catecholamine hormones from the adrenal medulla. Adrenaline, noradrenaline and dopamine produce the many changes in our body functions, to mention a few, blood glucose level rises, the circulation to the gut shuts down, more blood is diverted to muscles, sensitivity to pain reduces, memory and ability to think straight improves, sweat glands are switched on and the muscles tense, ready to act. These are only some of the inner reactions of our body which are all naturally designed to improve our chances of survival when faced with imminent danger. While the frontal lobes of our brain, where our speech, thoughts, emotions, skilled activities and judgement are formed, it also acts spontaneously bringing positive thoughts of survival and hope to the forefront of our thoughts. If faced with negative thoughts in the pit of our stomach we begin to experience the sinking feeling faced with fear of disaster and death. Very often faith and hope is recalled for strength and support, many of us remember consciously to evoke our faith in God. For someone who does not believe in God and has no faith, faced with imminent death, in those brief moments when your whole life suddenly flashes before you, when you may be thinking of your family members, your children, your passions, promises, your undisclosed secrets, your commitments, your unfulfilled desires, your sufferings, your achievements, your wealth, your instructions, your will, your legacies. You may have managed to live your life the way you want it. Now you only have memories flashing before you. Every single thing will be left to this world. What can you take with you? When you have no faith in God. Memories the self must remember, there is no control or escape over death our creator reminds us.

All will surely be gathered together for appointed meeting of a known Day

We have decreed death to you all, and we are not outstripped [30]

It is only a matter of time before the self experiences a situation, where its very own existence is in imminent danger or even near death. This can also be for our loved ones or a close friend whose life is now near its end. When their

---

[30] Quran(56;50 &60)

survival or lives hang in balance, faced with difficult moments and critical situations, when all human endeavours have failed to save the life facing death. Still, our self – our natural instincts demand help and support to save the life in need, we try making every effort to help and still maintain our faith and hope. If not, then the self is bound to feel helpless in the face of imminent death, which always brings pain and suffering to self and to next of kin. Who, are now sharing the experience of loss, and may be left to deal with the trauma of sudden death.

With regard to the personal belief and faith of the deceased, these would now be most needed by its body/soul for its comfort and solace in its next stage of existence? Remembering the soul does not die it is only extracted from the body to be carried into its next stage of existence.

It was God that gave life to the deceased. Who has passed away on it preordained time and place even to the exact moment of death in every detail.

Verily, Allah with him (Alone) is the knowledge of the hour, He sends down the rain, and knows that which is in the wombs. No person knows what he will earn tomorrow, and no person knows in what land he will die, Verily, Allah is All knower ,All –Aware

(Of things)[31]

Now, only the deceased's strength of faith in God would have made his/her last living moments less painful and even pleasant-in entering into the next stage of life where faith will

---

[31] Quran(31:34)

be confirmed to the appointed angels. To live we need to have faith in ourselves. It is the duty of every human to learn to have faith in his creator also.

Life without faith is like a body without a head, like a car without a steering wheel, a life lived without sense of direction and purpose. Only a life lived with faith is rewarded for its every good thought and action. Good intentions are sometime rewarded in this life or after death.

In this section, the **belief in God is the true purpose of human life.**

As human beings, we are created good and pure with natural awareness of good and evil.

We are a body mind and spirit that has intellect and conscious awareness, which has the freedom of choice. In life, there may come a moment in every mature and inquisitive mind to ask, why do I exist? What is the purpose of this life? To worship a deity is ingrained in human nature; it is also an attribute of the human soul. The correct understanding of these important questions can have a great impact on the mind that can change one's life. These answers can have a great influence on the mind – mind has the power to bring a change and develop a personality with the co-operation of one's spirit. A spirit that rules the body can follow the divine guidance. A body that yields to human passions and desires may allow for the destructions of the relationship between the body and spirit. The rule of spirit over the body inspires man to seek knowledge, and the knowledge practiced brings sparks of Intuitions to assist the spirit. The spirit obeys and lives this divine gift of life in harmony with the rest of creation. Having the correct knowledge and understanding is the key to understanding the true purpose of this life. One of the most important decisions that any human makes in this life is to believe in God. To have faith, to believe, to have values, that provides a structure that determines the trait of his personality. Wrong decisions will bring grave consequences to self and those under his or her influences. In the past, this search has been confined mainly to those who had the leisure and education for it – a small minority of people for most of history .Until the middle of the twentieth century, almost the only individuals who asked themselves serious searching questions were poets, philosophers and those engaged on a spiritual quest and in search for truth. People's lives were devoted to the quest and the meaning of their existence. To reach such a decision it requires true knowledge, a real conviction to form a faith. We all now live in communities; it is through communications that a community/society is formed. In order for the society to exist it must have common aims, beliefs, values and knowledge. Beliefs, faith, values, aspirations and knowledge cannot be physically extracted and inserted. The transmission of knowledge occurs by means of communication and in the form of education. Many definitions are given to the word education. The aim is always to shape the development of the human adult to its true potential. Education may be good or bad, its qualities will be relative to the virtue, wisdom and intelligence of the educators. The quality of education in a community varies with the quality of the beliefs and the ideals of that community, the best education being evidently that which prevails in a community which has the best beliefs, and values. A more conscious person must take the object view of the communities' education systems and its aims. The religious education is very important and belief in God is paramount. One must not simply adopt its family's religious beliefs or society's faith and cultural, traditions as their forefathers. Human logic demands proof of excellent ideals and values, a proof beyond doubt. To make an important decision one must have information and knowledge Educational growth is the urge of the human self not of the human body. Knowledge of human experience is passed on, its demonstrations inspire others to quest for knowledge. The goal of any knowledge is clarity of thought and understanding. Upon which we base our decisions and take action. When knowledge is applied correctly, it proves to be an asset, an advantage to its bearer. In any given situation, we follow the natural course of action simply first by our observations through our senses perceptions and then learning studying and remembering. Faith in God and religion is commonly inherited and passed on by parents or through our guardians. Sometimes it is through the strong influence of society and its culture. To have faith in God and to follow a religion is very personal, it becomes a believer's way of life. A belief in a religion will dictate its own divine rules, principles that have certain limits and restrictions. Religious faith can provide the individual with the true purpose of life and provide guidance in all aspects of their life. The divine guidance provides clear guideline for a man to live in peace with THE rest of his creation.

(It is a very serious decision, to believe or not to believe in God – yes or- no will carry grave consequences in this life and for the life after, it has to be made with visual proof to convince our intellect with our sense perceptions) First one has to be convinced that there is God.

This decision is not reached easily, it requires independence, free will, a firm commitment and real conviction. To reach this decision, knowledge is required; to gain knowledge, is to experience with one's own sense perception, first by the realization of our conscious awareness, second the acceptance of spirit-soul. All of these faculties are used in the learning process. Our memory is a wonderful faculty, without it, one is unable to make the correct decision. To make a decision we need to draw upon our knowledge. It is our natural instinct to acquire knowledge about our self, and where we are, and how we got here, what we believe in. First is to believe in a creator. Every man first tries to apply logic and reason to understand things. Sometimes due to our intellectual weakness, we simply assume that everything must be comparable to our previous experiences and understanding, we also rely on our imagination which is incapable of grappling with the absolutes with the universal concepts. The human mind cannot perceive what God is made of. it is simply beyond human comprehension to even imagine of God's shape or form, God has always been everywhere, God is first and the last, the following revelation is from God, (God has ninety-nine Arabic names which are all his qualities and attributes, the Name Allah encapsulates them all).

Allah! (None has the right to be worship but he), the ever living, (and one who sustains and protects all that exists.) Neither slumber nor sleep overtakes him. To him belongs whatever is in the heavens and whatever is on

earth. Who is he that can intercede with him except with him permission? He knows what happens to them (his creatures) in this world, and what will happen to them in the Hereafter. And they will never encompass anything of his knowledge except that what he wills. His footstool (chair) extends over the heavens and earth, and he feels no fatigue in guarding and preserving them.

And He is Most High the Most Great[32]

Some people will keep asking questions until they come to ask, God created the universe, but who created God?

Prophet Muhammed, may peace be upon him, replied whoever has thoughts like this should simply declare, I believe in God. Seek God's help and desist from such thoughts. The human mind has limitations and our human perspective is deficient.

We need to realize that we are dealing here with a matter of faith, in other words, a matter which transcends the limitations of human reason. The human mind accepts the existence of a creator. Reason has to accept the truth. Our minds intuitively seek guidance about God, our natural inclination is to worship our creator. Our intellect certainly recognizes his creation but we are not capable of comprehending his infinite attributes. Looking back at human history, thousands of years before when young prophet Ibrahim lived with his father in a community teeming with misguided people who all worshiped idols and other deities. Ibrahim questioned their beliefs, used his senses perception

---

[32] Quran(2:255)

and intellect and asked for guidance and the creator confirmed, and replied with this revelation;

And of his signs are the night and the day, the sun and the moon. Prostrate not yourselves before the sun or the moon, but prostrate yourselves before Allah who created them; if it is, in truth, Him whom you worship[33]

Our creator reminds us regarding our senses,

And Allah has brought you out from the wombs of your mothers while you know nothing. And he gave you hearing, sight and hearts that you might give thanks (to Allah).[34]

Our creator reminds us regarding his creation, the signs for people who understand,

And in the alternation of night and day and the provision (rain) that Allah sends down from the sky , and revives therewith the earth after its death ,and in the turning about the winds (i.e. sometimes towards the east or north, sometimes towards the south or west sometimes bringing glad tidings of rain and sometimes bringing the torment) are the signs for a people who understand?[35]

Knowledge is drawn from three main sources, nature, past civilizations, and perfectly preserved original divine revelations.

One does not need to search for the knowledge or the proof of God in the historical records or any science manual the visual proof of God's creations has always been present, the universe.

---

[33] Quran((41:37)

[34] Quran(16:78)

[35] Quran(45:5)

To believe in God we only need to look at his creation of the whole universe and our self.

Only our creator can make the following statements; about his creations, of human soul's temptations, and death. All worship and praise is for Allah.

We have not created the heaven and the earth, and all that lies between them out of fun[36]

We have determined the stations of the moon, so that (after its wondering) it returns as a dried up inflorescent spike of dates[37]

Neither can the sun overtake the moon, nor do the nights outpace the day;

Each of them keeps coursing in its orbit[38]

He merges night into day, and merges day into night; and has full knowledge of whatsoever is in your hearts[39]

Every soul will know the taste of death. We tempt you with evil and good as a trial; and to us you will return.[40]

Say (O Muhammad to mankind) if the ocean turned to ink for writing down the colloquy of my lord the ocean itself would be exhausted to hear the words (and wonders) of my Lord come to end, even if we brought another like it for replenishment"[41]

Most human's minds acknowledge the existence of a creator. Reason cannot escape from such thoughts. Every

---

[36] Quran(21:16)
[37] Quran(36;39)
[38] Quran(36:40)
[39] Quran:57-6
[40] Quran:21-35
[41] Quran:18-109

inquisitive mind consequently seeks guidance and inquiries about his creator and the spirit within which provides him with the natural inclination to worship.

The following very old Archaeologist findings confirms this humans desire to build a place of worship even many thousands of years before.

The German archaeologist, Professor Klaus Schmidt (Dec 11 1953- 20 July 2014) was a pioneer of excavation who discovered the Ancient Gobelitepe potbelly Hill also known as" the zero point in history" in the eastern Turkish province of Sanliurfa in archaeological findings, also found a temple, a place of worship built 11,500 years ago, A Staggering 7000 before the grand pyramids 6000 year before Stone Henge took shape. These ancient grand monuments are the lasting evidence of those bygone civilizations who did not worship one true God. (Allah) The simple drawings and engraving on the stones reflect their beliefs, values and their understanding of mortal life and their misconception of human soul and their desire of re-incarnation. The pharaohs committed a great sin by creating idols gods; some pharaohs considered they were divine and demanded to worship by their subject and some imposed blood sacrifices. Believing in another deity is the one grave sin which God does not forgive. He promises to all true believers that he may forgive all their sins but not one who holds no belief in God, and those who ascribe partners to God. The following revelations reminds us,

And your lord creates whatsoever he wills and chooses, no choice have they (in any matter) Glorified is Allah and exalted above all that they associate (as partners with him)[42]

And the lord knows what their breast conceals and what they reveal.

And He is Allah; la I laha illa huwa (none has the right to be worshipped but he) His are all the parise and thanks both in the first and in this word and in the hereafter and Him is the decision and to Him shall all return.[43]

Say (O Muhammad tell me if Allah made the night continuous for you till the day of resurrection which God besides Allah could bring you light? Will you not then hear?[44]

---

[42] Quran(28:68)
[43] Quran(28-69&70)
[44] Quran(28-71)

First Human – Adam

Many scientists use it only as a figure of speech that Adam walked the earth 209,000 years ago. To calculate the age of the Y chromosome, researchers multiplied data on the age of the fathers having their first child with the number of mutations they uncovered. In today's modern times via the internet, we are very fortunate to be able to access and share information so quickly, and benefit from the endeavours of archaeologists fascinating discoveries of the past civilizations that lived thousands of years before. The scientists are able to perform DNA tests and by comparing the chromosomes, the archaeologists are able to perform radio carbon dating tests on cave drawings and pictures.

In one of the Britannia history manuals, it is stated that it was thanks to many years of hard work by a dedicated team of archaeologists, Louis Leakey and his wife Mary. Louis Leaky, a pioneer of the search for human origins in Africa, was attracted to Olduvai by its abundance of fossils and animal bones, which led him to believe that it might also have been home to hominids. After spending almost thirty years uncovering thousands of fossils and stone artefacts, he and his wife Mary were, in 1959 , rewarded by the discovery of a 1.75 million-year-old hominid skull. They nicknamed this first fossil evidence of Australopithecus Boisei, their "Dear Boy ".

It proves some kind of homo type creature lived on this earth thousands of years in the past. These archaeological finds are very important pieces of human history. These historical finds provide many answers to our past. We need to remind ourselves that these finds only provide part of the answer when it comes to human fossils, all other historical artefacts that form the basis of very interesting theories concerning origin and the history of man, are theories only. The seeker of the truth must take notice and learn from the statement of his creator; man cannot ignore his own history described in the divine revelation, in which there cannot be any doubt. The Noble Quran a Miracle from Allah to his last prophet Muhammad.

And this Quran is not such as could be ever be produced by other than Allah (Lord of the heavens and earth) but it is confirmation of|(the revelation) which was before it the Taurat (Torah) and Injil (Gospel) and explanations of the book (law decreed for mankind) – wherein there is no doubt – from the lord of the mankind Jinn and all that exists[45]

Verily, We it is We who have sent down the Quran and surely we will guard it (from corruption)[46]

This verse is a challenge to mankind and everyone is obliged to believe in the miracle of this Quran. It is a clear fact that more than 1400 years have elapsed and not a single word of this Quran has been changed, although the disbelievers tried their utmost to change it in every way but they failed miserably in their efforts. As it is mentioned in the holy verse;

---

[45] Quran(10:37)
[46] Quran(15:9)

we will guard it by Allah has guarded it on the contrary to all the other holy books, the Torah and Gospel have been corrupted in the form of additions and subtractions or alteration to the original text.

Human history begins with **Adam**, Adam is an Arabic word for man, also as in Hebrew. He was the progenitor of the human race. Angels were sent to earth to collect soil for Adam. It was red, white, brown and black. It came from the mountains and valleys from infertile deserts and lush fertile plains and all natural varieties. The descendants of Adam were destined to be as diverse as the handful of soil from which their ancestor was created all to have different appearances, attributes and qualities.

O mankind! We have created you from a male and a female, and made you into nations and tribes that you may know one another. Verily, the most honourable of you in the sight of Allah is that believer who is most pious.[47]

Man's interest in his own origin has always been present in every civilization, probably because of his inquisitive and curious nature to know and learn of his past, which has helped him to make many improvements to his life on earth. Our creator now reminds us to heed and learn from the monuments left by the past civilizations that mock the prophets and ignored their teachings, and worshipped idols.

Do they not travel in the land and see what the end of those before them was? They were superior to them in strength and they tilled the earth and populated it in greater

---

[47] Quran(49:13)

numbers than these pagans have done and there came to them their Messengers with clear proofs, surely Allah wronged them not, but they use to wrong themselves [48]

Seth was the third son of the prophet Adam. When he was born, his father the prophet Adam had attained the age of 130 years Allah conferred upon him the honour of prophethood after his father. Many prophets came before the last prophet Muhammad.

Only twenty-five of the following names in chronological order are mentioned in the Quran. **And, indeed we have sent messengers before you O Mohammad some them we have related to you their story and of some we have not related to you their story, and it was not given to any messenger that he should bring a sign except by the leave of Allah, But, when comes the commandment of Allah, the matter will be decided with truth and the follower of falsehood will then be lost.**[49]

Then when the messenger's come to them with clear proofs they were glad (and proud) with that which they had of knowledge (of worldly things) and that at which they use to mock, surrounded them (with punishments) [50]

Ibrahim was neither a Jew no a Christian, but he was true Muslim, who worshiped none but Allah[51]

---

[48] Quran(30:9)
[49] Quran(40:78)
[50] Quran(40:83)
[51] Quran(3:67)

Arabic	English
Adam	Adam
Sheth	Seth
Idris	Idris
Nuh	Noah
Hud	Hud
Saleh	Saleh
Lut	Lot
Abrahim	Abraham
Ismail	Ishmael
Ishaq	Isaac
Yaqub	Jacob
Yusuf	Joseph
Shuaib	Shuaib
Dawud	David
Sulaiman	Solomon
Iyas	Elias
Alyasa	Elisha
Musa	Moses
Aziz	Ezra
Ayyub	Job
Dhul- kifil	Dhul-Kifil
Yunus	Jonah
Zakariya	Zachariah
yahya	John
Isa	Jesus
Mohammad	Muhammad

Say O Muhammad we believe in Allah and in what has been sent down to us and what was sent down to Ibrahim, Ismail, Ishaq, Yaqub and alsbat (the offspring of the twelve sons of yaqub) and what was given to Moses and Jesus and the prophets from the lord we make no distinctions between one another among them and to him(Allah) we have submitted in Islam[52]

Whoever seeks a religion other than Islam, it will never be accepted of him, and in the hereafter he will be one of the losers[53]

The holy Quran reminds us of the outcomes endured by the nations that refused to believe in God's prophets and their true message. Over the centuries eventually these nations were punished by God they were destroyed with calamities and disasters. It up to us to accept and learn from the following words of the holy Quran;

Perfect wisdom (this Quran) but (the preaching of) of warner's benefit them not [54]

The people of Nuh (Noah) denied (their Messenger) before them. The reject our slave and said; "A madman" and he was insolently rebuked and threatened.[55]

Then he invoked his lord (saying) "I have been overcome so help (me)"[56]

---

[52] Quran(3:84)
[53] Quran(3:85)
[54] Quran(54:5)
[55] Quran(54:9)
[56] Quran(54:10)

So, we open the gates of the heaven and water pouring forth[57]

And we caused springs to gush forth from the earth so the water of the heaven and the earth met for the matter predestined[58]

And we carried him on a ship made of planks and nails[59]

And (people) denied their prophet Hud then how terrible was my torment and my warnings?[60]

Verily, we sent against them a furious wind of harsh voice on a day of evil omen and continuous calamity [61]

Plucking out men as if they were uprooted stems of date palms.[62]

Then, how terrible was my torment and my warnings?[63]

And we have indeed made the Quran easy to understand and remember, and then is there any that will remember or receive admonition?[64]

Thamud's people also denied the warnings[65]

And they said" A man alone among us shall we follow him? Truly then we should be in error and distress or madness![66]

---

[57] Quran(54:11)
[58] Quran(54:12)
[59] Quran(54:13)
[60] Quran(54:18)
[61] Quran(54:19)
[62] Quran(54:20)
[63] Quran(54:21)
[64] Quran(54:22)
[65] Quran(54:23)
[66] Quran(54:24)

Is it that the reminder is sent to him prophet Salih alone from amongs us? Nay he is an insolent liar! [67]

Tomorrow they will come to know who the liar the insolent one is[68]

Verily, we are sending the she camel as a test for them. So watch them O Salih and be patient![69]

And informed them the water is to be shared between her and them each one's right to drink being established by turn[70]

But they called their comrade and he took a sword and killed (her) [71]

How terrible were my torments and my warnings?[72]

Verily we sent against them a single torment awful cry and they became like stubble of fold builder,[73]

The people of lut (lot) denied the warnigns[74]

Verily we sent against them a violent storm of stones which destroyed them all except the family of Lut (Lot) them we saved in the last hour of the night [75]

And indeed, warning came to the people Firaun (pharaoh) through Moses and Aaron.[76]

---

[67] Quran(54:25)
[68] Quran(54:26)
[69] Quran(54:27)
[70] Quran(54:28)
[71] Quran(54:29)
[72] Quran(54:30)
[73] Quran(54:31)
[74] Quran(54:33)
[75] Quran(54:34)
[76] Quran(54:41)

They denied all our signs, so we seized them with a seizure of the all mighty all capable and omnipotent[77]

Are the disbelievers (O Quraysh) better than these nations of Noah, Lut, Salih and the people of pharaoh who were destroyed? Or have you immunity (Against our torment) in the divine scriptures?[78]

---

[77] Quran(54:42)

[78] Quran(54:43)

Ancient Civilizations

Mesopotamians', Indus Valley, Egyptians, Mayan, Chinese, Greeks, Persians, Romans, have been the main civilizations that populated the earth in greater numbers and have left their great landmarks, inventions and achievements, when, where, what was their beliefs, how did they practice their faith, and what became of them, some brief historical information is presented to benefit the reader. Some of these civilizations lived without the benefit of true knowledge and some directly mocked their prophets, some stubbornly followed the practices of their forefathers in worshiping idols and some simply refused to believe in one true God.

The history of human civilisation begins with ***Mesopotamia,*** the cradle of ancient civilization. Here the earliest cities in world history appeared about 3500 BC. The contribution they made to early writing, is described as pictographic which gives some idea to the archaeologists that they had some form of government, welfare, religion, economy and society, science and technology, art and culture. It would take a complete volume dedicated to their history to fully describe and report all the great achievements of the ancient Sumerian people. Mesopotamia is a Greek word meaning between the rivers, this is vast dry plain through which two great rivers flow, the Euphrates and Tigris. Today, the rivers unite before they empty into the Persian

Gulf, but in ancient times, the sea came much further inland, and they flowed into it as two separate streams. Sumerian speakers lived near the great rivers and it was they who built the first cities. Their language therefore became the first to be written down in world history. The Mesopotamians developed mathematics to a more advanced level than any contemporary people, and in so doing laid many of the foundations for modern mathematics. Mesopotamian scribes produced detailed mathematical tables, as well as texts posing advance mathematical problems. From these we know that they developed a member system based on sixty which has given us the sixty-minute hour, the twenty-four hour day and 360 degree circle. The Sumerian calendar was based on the seven day week. Their number system, alone in the ancient world, had place markers to denote values, as modern mathematics (as in 3,333 when the number 3 represents 3,000, 300, 30 and 3 respectively).

A major branch of Mesopotamian science was astronomy. Mesopotamian priests produced astronomical tables and could predict eclipses and solstices. They worked out a twelve month calendar based on the cycles of the moon. Mesopotamian astronomical knowledge was later to have a major influence on Greek astronomy. Mesopotamian religion was polytheistic, more than 2000 gods and goddesses have been identified. For the Sumerians, it was Enlil, the Sky God. The chief of the gods varied from period to period. The Mesopotamians conceived of the material world as being deeply bound up with the divine. Ancient Mesopotamians must surely be the most influential civilization in earth's history. They were the first to build cities, use potter's wheels, develop writing, use bronze in large quantities, evolve complex bureaucracies, organise proper armies. All subsequent Western civilizations were ultimately built largely upon the foundations laid here. Mesopotamian civilization deeply influenced the societies in Syria, Palestine and Egypt.

Indus Valley civilization was an ancient civilization located in what is Pakistan and north-west India today, on the fertile flood plain of the Indus River and its vicinity.

Evidence of religious practices in this area date back approximately to 5500. Farming settlements began around 4000 BCE and around 3000 BCE there appeared the first signs of urbanization. By 2600BEC, dozens of towns and cities had been established, and between 2500 and 2000 BCE Indus Valley Civilization was at its peak. Two cities in particular have been excavated at the sites of Mohenjo-Daro the lower Indus and at Harappa further upstream. The evidence suggests they had highly developed systems, city life .The social conditions of the citizens were comparable to Sumerian and superior to the contemporary Babylonians and Egyptians. These cities displayed a well-planned urbanization system. The Indus Civilization had a writing system which today still remains a mystery because all attempts to decipher it have failed. This is one of the reasons why the Indus Valley civilization is of the least known. By 1800BCE the Indus Valley Civilization saw the beginning of the their decline, examples of the their writing system found in pottery amulets, carved stamps, seals, copper tables. Standardized weight and measures used for trade and taxation purpose fell out of use and the cities were gradually abandoned. This civilization has raised many great unanswered questions of archaeologists and historians. Why did this civilization considering its sophistication not spread beyond the Indus Valley? In contrast to contemporary Egyptian and Mesopotamian civilizations, Indus Valley lack any monumental palaces, even though excavated cities indicate the society possessed the requisite engineering knowledge. This would suggest if any religious ceremonies were performed it may have been confined to home or small temples. A few thousand seals have been discovered in Indus Valley showing some 400 pictographs, too few for the language to have been phonetic. Several sites have been proposed by Marshall (1931) and later scholars also proposed that it was possibly devoted to religious purposes. However, at present only the Great Bath at Mohenjo-Daro is widely thought to have been used as place for ritual purification. The funerary practices of the Harappan civilization is marked by its diversity with the evidence of a supine burial, a fractional burial, in which the body is reduced to skeletal remains by exposure to elements before final interment, even cremation. The religion and belief system of the Indus Valley people have received considerable attention, especially from the view of identifying precursors to deities and religious practices of the Indian religion that later developed in the area, which is open to varying interpretations and the fact that the Indus script remains un-deciphered. The conclusions are partly and selectively based on a retrospective view from a much later Hindu perspective. Today many scholars believe that the collapse of the Indus civilization was caused by drought, and decline in trade with Egypt and Mesopotamia. The five points of our interest can be determined from the above information, when, where, what religious beliefs they followed, what faith they practiced, and what may have caused there demise. It is clear, that the worshipping of the one true God was not practiced by the Indus Valley civilization for whatever their reasons.

Abraham was neither a Jew nor a Christian but he was a true Muslim who worshipped none but Allah-Alone he was not of those who worship idols[79]

Such a divine guidance was sent to them, this was clearly ignored out of ignorance, which has become clear from the Holy Scriptures given to subsequent prophets that came after Abraham and before Moses. Our creator, Allah, sent messengers to every nation for guidance.

The Ancient **Egyptians** were also one of the oldest civilizations, they are known for their prodigious culture, the ever standing pyramids and the sphinx, the pharaohs, a majestic civilization that resided by the banks of the River Nile. The civilization coalesced around 3150 BC according to conventional Egyptian chronology. It is not possible to ascertain if the divine revelations from the past had reached this ancient civilization, it is certain from the practices of polytheism, the message brought by the prophets before them was not followed, because all of the prophets brought the same message every time, to only worship one true God. The historical findings clearly show they worshiped many deities. Once more our aim is to determine from their practices of the five main key points adapted in the everyday life by this civilization – when, where, their religion, what faith

---

[79] Quran(3:67)

they practiced and what finally became of them. The Egyptian civilization has made many contributions to early inventions, they were the pioneers in the field of making things, like, glass, linen, first invention of paper from tree leaves (papyrus tree) ink pot, the calendar, the clock, geometry and the alphabet, refinements of dress and ornaments, furniture and dwellings, some of the everyday useful things that we now take for granted. They also organized the first peaceful and orderly form of government: first united nation, centralised government, census and post, primary and secondary education, technical training, office and administration, Medical science. For thousands of years ancient Egyptians already had a thorough understanding of painkillers and laid the foundation for modern-day medical means of pain relief. They had the knowledge of the narcotics in natural herbs like the water lily and lotus, cannabis, the poppy and the mandrake. They used these natural remedies to control pain long before Europeans figured out the natural powers of such herbs. They also composed literature concerning astrology, metallurgy, weaving and cooking. The Egyptians were the father of historiography their historians accompanied the pharaohs to the battlefield and recoded their achievements. The Rosetta stone is its classic example. By deciphering it, the French palaeographer, Champollion, (who accompanied Napoleon on his expedition to Egypt 1800 AD) had discerned many facts regarding the Egyptian's civilization. Clearly the Ancient Egyptians have immortalised their name in the annals of history due to their art and architecture. The Pyramids are a classic example of it. The tomb of the Egyptian Pharaohs are known as pyramids.

(The people of Egypt believed that after death, the soul returned back to the body.)

Among the pyramids of Egypt, the pyramid built by Pharaoh Josher at Sakkara is the oldest.

The famous and largest Pyramid of Khufu was built at Giza. This is regarded as one of the Seven Wonders of the World. This 481 feet Pyramid is built of over thirteen acres of land 2,300,000 pieces of stone were used in it. The weight of each piece of stone is 2.5 tons. Nearly twenty years were spent in building this pyramid. Religion played a vital role in the life of the Egyptians. From the beginning, they believed in polytheism they worshipped around 2200 gods and goddesses. They attached divinity to creatures and worshipped them. Their crocodile god was known as Sibek, the cat god was called pashat and the jackal god was named Anubis. Freedom of choice in matter of life-style and religion must have prevailed for some, clearly a majority of the population were not only defiant but totally misguided about God, life, and life after death. Their rulers must be held responsible for their choice of polytheism and not monotheism. It was to the pharaoh prophet Moses came with the divine revelation. Moses was born in 1593 BCE in Egypt son of Am Ram, meaning the man of the true God.

And indeed we sent Moses with our signs, proof and evidence saying bring out your people from darkness into light, and remind them of the annals of Allah. Truly, therein are proofs and signs for every patient, thankful person.[80]

---

[80] Quran(14:5)

And remember when Moses said to his people; call to mind Allah's favours to. When he delivered you from the pharaoh who was afflicting you with horrible torment and were slaughtering your sons and sparing your women and in it was a tremendous trial from your lord.[81]

The ancient **Mayan** civilization flourished in Central America from about 2600BC. The ancient Mayans were culturally richer when compared to many of the contemporary civilizations. The Mayans and Aztecs both built pyramids, many of which are larger them those in Egypt. Excavations of Mayna sites have unearthed plazas, palaces, temples and pyramids, as well as courts for playing the ball games that were ritually and politically significant to Mayan culture. They were deeply religious and worshiped various gods related to nature, including the god of the sun, the moon, rain and corn. At the top of Maya society were the kings or "Kuhul ajaw" (holy lords) who claimed to be related to gods and followed hereditary succession. They were thought to serve as mediators between the gods and people on earth, and performed the elaborate religious ceremonies and rituals so important to Maya culture. The Classic Maya built many of their temples and palaces in a stepped pyramid shape, decorating them with elaborate reliefs and inscriptions. These structures have earned the Maya their reputations as the great artists of Mesoamerica. Guided by their religious ritual they also made significant advances in

---

[81] Quran(14:6)

mathematics and astronomy including the use of the zero and the development of a complex calendar based on 365 days.

Serious exploration of classic Maya sites began in the 1820s. By the early to mid-twentieth century, a small portion of their system of hieroglyph writing had been deciphered and more about their history had become known. Most of what historians know about the Maya comes from what remains of their architecture and art, including stone carving and inscriptions of their building and monuments. From the late eighth through to the end of the ninth century, something unknown happened to shake the Maya civilization to its foundation. One by one, the classic cities in the southern lowland were abandoned and by A.D.900 Maya civilization in the region collapsed. The reason for this mysterious decline is not known, though scholars developed several competing theories. Such as overpopulation, overuse of land, endemic warfare and droughts may have played a part in the downfall of the Maya in the southern lowland. In the highlands of Yucatan, a few Maya cities such Chic hen Itza , Uzmal Maya pan continued to flourish in the post-classic period A.D 900-1500 . By the time the Spanish invaders arrived however, most Maya were living in agricultural villages; their great cities buried under green rainforests. Descendants of the Maya live in parts of Central America to this day.

The Chinese nation is not only the most populous but also one the oldest in the world. China is an East Asian country with a large territory, a huge population and an ancient history. With written records dating back 4,000 years, it is also recognized as one of the four great ancient civilizations of the world, together with ancient Indus Valley, Mesopotamia, and Mayans.

It is the only ancient civilization that has continued to this day. According to legend, the primitive tribes that inhabited the middle and upper reaches of the Yellow River were unified into two powerful tribes under the Yellow Emperor and Fiery Emperor, and began their push southward 5000 years ago. After years of warfare, they conquered the Sanmiao and Jiuli tribes active in south China under the leadership of Chi You. Part of the defeated tribe was incorporated into the tribes under the Yellow and Fiery Emperors to became a component part the of the Han people, which marked the beginning of the Chinese nation. Archaeological studies have revealed that around 5000 years ago, the Chinese entered the stage of patriarchal society. Villages began to appear, also the initial form of cities began to become evident. Extensive communities indicated that the population at the time had reached a fairly large size and agriculture had made great headway. The earliest discoveries took place during this period.

Shen Nong tried and tested various kinds of wild plants to select crops appropriate to be cultivated for food and herbal medicine to cure disease. The Yellow Emperor was credited with the invention of the compass, which helped him defeat Chi You, however, more importantly, the appearance of chariots greatly reduced labour intensity. Lei Su ,wife of the Yellow Emperor discovered silk making by raising silkworms, and produced the first garments, which allowed the ancient people to bid goodbye to the period when they wore animal skins and tree leaves Ancient China enjoyed developing agriculture and advanced irrigation systems and independent traditions of medicine and advanced botanical knowledge. China's four great inventions, the compass, gunpowder, movable type printing and papermaking, not only changed the world but also accelerated the evolution of world history. China was rich in ceramics and silk textiles, invented alcohol, cannons and many more. China also kept the world's most detailed earliest astronomical records. The first people to take note of such astronomical phenomena as comets sunspots and new stars were all Chinese. It was also the Chinese who produced the first advanced astronomical observatory apparatus of the time. In metallurgy, China long held a leading position. When Europeans still could not turn out a single piece of cast iron in the 14th century, Chinese people had already produced cast iron on an industrial scale four centuries earlier.

In the field of thought, Confucius, the founder of Confucianism, not only had far-reaching significance for china, but whole of the East and Southeast Asia. Confucianism (also known as Rujia ju chia meaning the school of scholar) is the body of thought that arguably had the most enduring effect on Chinese life. Its written legacy lies in the Confucian classic which later became the foundation of traditional society. Confucius 551- 479 BC or Kongzi (Master Kong) looked back to the early days of Zhou dynasty for and ideal socio-political order. He believed that the only effective system of government necessitated prescribed relationships of each individual "let the ruler be ruler and the subject as subject ". Furthermore, he contended that a king must be virtuous in order to rule a state properly. To Confucius the functions of government and social stratification were facts of life to be sustained by ethical values, the ideal man was the Junzi which translated as gentleman or superior person.

As the potential leader of a nation, the son of the ruler is raised to express superior ethical and moral positions while gaining inner peace through virtue.

Mencius 371-289BC or Mengzi formulated his teachings directly in response to Confucius. The effect of the combined work of Confucius, the codifier and interpreter of a system of relationships based on ethical behaviour and Mencius the synthesizer and the developer of applied Confucianism thought, was to provide traditional Chinese society with a comprehensive framework by which to order virtually every aspect of life. There were many accretions to the body of Confucian thought, both immediately and over the millennia, from within and from out of the Confucian school. Interpretations adapted to contemporary society allowed flexibility within Confucianism, while the fundamental system of modelled behaviour from ancient text formed its philosophical core. Diametrically opposed to Mencius, in regards to human nature was the interpretation of Xunzi 330-237BC and after these interpretations, Confucian followed. Xunzi preached that man is not innately good; he asserted that goodness is attainable only through training one's desires and conduct.

Fajia Fa-chia, the school of law doctrine was formulated by Li kui Shang yang 338BC Han Feizi 233BC and Li Si 208BC who maintained that human nature was incorrigibly selfish, accordingly, the only way to preserve the social order was to impose discipline from above, and to see to a strict enforcement of laws. The legalists exalted the state above all, seeking its prosperity and martial powers over the welfare of the common people. Legalism greatly influenced the philosophical basis for the imperial form of government. During the Han Dynasty, the most practical elements of Confucianism and legalism were taken to form a sort of synthesis marking the creation of new form of government that would remain largely intact until the late nineteenth century. In the history of China there have been many dynasties that have ruled China - from the ancient Neolithic (8500- 2070c) to the Qin dynasty (221-206 BC) to the Han Dynasty (206- 220AD) and many more in between that lead us up to the modern Republic of China (1912-1949). The late Joseph Needham, historian of China science and technology and professor at Cambridge University, once said that people must remember that China was way ahead of the west in almost every discipline on science and technology, from chart-making to gunpowder.

In order to have a better understanding of the ancient Chinese civilization the above findings provide us with a clear idea of the four main points of our interest when , where , what they believed and what they practiced, more importantly their impressive inventions and achievements for a practical life. When it comes to the most important point of clear belief in God and religion it is not clear. It has always been difficult for a westerner to have a clear understanding of Chinese religion. Religion as it is commonly defined today in the modern secularized societies as a domain of thinking and religious practices of a particular faith. The Chinese religious practices and philosophical ideas from

Confucianism, Daoism and Buddhism, cannot be easily classified.

Ancient Greece was a civilization belonging to a period of Greek history that lasted from the archaic period of the 8th to 6th centuries BC to the end of antiquity (600AD)

Classical Greek culture, especially philosophy, had a powerful influence on the Roman Empire which carried a version of it to many parts of the Mediterranean basin and Europe.

Traditionally the archaic period of ancient Greece is considered to begin with orientalising influence which among other things brought the alphabetic script to Greece marking the beginning of Greek literature, Homer, Hesiod. The end of the Dark Ages is also frequently dated 776BC, the year of the first Olympic Games. The Archaic period gives way to the classical around 500 BC, in turn succeeded by the Hellenistic period at the death of Alexander the Great in 323 BC. The historical period of ancient Greece is unique in world history as the first period attested directly in proper historiography , while earlier ancient history or proto history is known by much more circumstantial evidence, such as annals or king lists and pragmatic epigraphy. Herodotus is widely known as the father of history, his histories are eponymous of the entire field written between the 450s and 420s BC. Herodotus' work reaches about a century into the past discussing 6th century historical figures such as Darius 1 of Persia Cambyses 11 and Psamtik 111 and alluding to some 8th century ones such as Candaules. Herodotus was succeeded by authors such as Thucydides Xenophon Demosthenes Plato and Aristotle. Most of these authors were either Athenians or pro Athenians, which is why far more is known about the history and politics of Athens than those of many other cities. Their scope is further limited by a focus on political, military and diplomatic history, ignoring economic and social history. From about the 9th century BC written records begin to appear. Greece was divided into many small, self-governing communities; a pattern largely dictated by Greek geography, every island, valley and plain is cut off from its neighbours by the sea and mountain ranges. The Levantine war c 710- c 650 is the earliest documented war of the ancient Greek period. It was fought between the important poleis, city states, of Chalcis and Eretria over the fertile Levantine plain of Eubuea, both cities seem to have suffered a decline as a result of a long war, though Chalcis was the victor. Rapidly increasing population in the 8th and 7th centuries had resulted in emigration of many Greeks to and from colonies in Magna Graecia, southern Italy, and Sicily, Asia Minor and further afield. The emigration effectively ceased in the 6th century by which time the Greek world had culturally and linguistically became much larger than the area of present day Greece. The weaken state of the heartland of Greece coincided with the rise of Macedon led by Philip 11. In twenty years Philip unified his kingdom expanded it north and west at the expense of Illyrian tribes and then conquered Thessaly and Thrace. His success stemmed from his innovative reform to the Macedon army. Philip intervened repeatedly in the affairs of the southern city-states culminating in his invasion of 338 BC. Alexander son and successor of Philip continued the war. Alexander defeated Darius III of Persia and completely destroyed the Achaemenes Empire annexing it to Macedon and earning himself the epithet 'the Great' When Alexander died in323 BC, Greek power and influence was at its zenith. Initially many Greek city-states seem to have had petty kingdoms, there was often a city official carrying some residual ceremonial functions for the king, Basilar. Athens fell under a tyranny in the second half of the 6th century. When this tyranny was ended, the Athenians founded the world's first democracy as a radical solution to prevent the aristocracy regaining power. Ancient Greece consisted of several hundred relatively independent city-states, poleis. On the one hand the ancient Greeks had no doubt that they were 'one people' they had the same religion same basic culture and same language. Many Greeks migrated to Alexandria, Antioch and many other new Hellenistic cities founded in Alexander's wake as far away as what are now Afghanistan and Pakistan. The Greek peninsula came under Roman rules during the 146 BC conquest of Greece after the battle of Corinth, Macedonia became a Roman province.

Only free, land owning, native born men could be citizens entitled to full protection of the law in a city state. Slaves had no power or status, they had the right to have a family and own property, subject to their masters' goodwill and permission, but they had no political rights.

City-states legally owned slaves. These public slaves had a larger measure of independence than slaves owned by families living on their own and performing specialised tasks.

For most of Greek history, education was private except in Sparta. During the Hellenistic period some city-states established public schools, only the wealthy families could afford a teacher. Boys learned to read and write and quote literature. Girls also learned to read write and do simple arithmetic so they could manage the household. They almost never received education after childhood. Ancient Greek philosophies focused on the role of reason and inquiry, in many ways it had an important influence on modern philosophy as well as modern science. The art of ancient Greece has exercised an enormous influence on the culture of many countries from ancient times until the present, particularly in the area of sculpture and architecture. The achievements of one great mind tower above many others even to this day. It can be said that Eratosthenes is most widely known as a famous Greek mathematician, geographer, astronomer and historian. Several astronomers and mathematicians before and after Eratosthenes tried to accurately measure the circumference of the earth but it was Eratosthenes that came through. He found the circumference of the earth to nearly 250,000 stadia 25,000 miles. Eratosthenes observed that the sun shone directly down a well high noon on the day of summer solstice in Syene and that it cast a shadow in Alexandria directly south where he was. To calculate the circumference of the earth, Eratosthenes measured the angle of the shadow to the earth. Until he realised this, Eratosthenes believed that the sun was so far away that its rays were parallel.

Greek mythology consists of stories belonging to the ancient Greeks concerning their gods and heroes the nature of the world and the origin and significance of their religious practices. The main Greek gods were the twelve Olympians, Zeus, his wife, Hera, Poseidon, Ares, Hermes, Hephaestus, Aphrodite, Athena, Apollo, Artemis, and Dionysus. The

Parthenon, a temple dedicated to Athena located on the Acropolis in is one of the most representative symbols of the culture and sophistication of the ancient Greeks its great pillars are still standing overlooking the great city of Athens.

From these records of ancient Greeks, it is easily possible to determine the five points of our interest when, where, what they believed, what they religious practice were and their faith.

In the light of their knowledge and wisdom, they still remain deprived of the true knowledge of one true God and their creator who sent many prophets and messenger to every nation that ever lived. Why they did not practice the divine teaching – only to worship one God, we cannot say, following these civilizations , there came subsequent prophets with holy scriptures from these we learn their final outcome, (From the Holly Quran). This is referred to in the conclusion in the following pages. (Of all civilizations)

Persian Civilization

As with the ancient civilizations like Mesopotamia, Indus Valley, Egyptian, Mayan, Chinese, Greek referred to in the preceding pages, it would need the efforts of many volumes of historical records to fully describe all the great achievements of the Persian civilisation that wielded a mighty military power that the ancient world had ever assembled. Only a few key events are mentioned here. Some knowledge of the main points such as when, where and what they believed and what they worshipped and the impact that the subsequent true knowledge had over this vast population. The divine message of one true God had its lasting impact over this nation and its enduring effect on its culture up until the present day

In the past centuries, once a vast and dominant empire was described as the 'Persian civilisation', in our time it is known as Iran. In the last fourteen hundred years, with the spread of Islam, Iran has yielded many important scholars who have spread great influence on the followers of Islam. Persian poetry, literature, philosophy has had great impact on the Muslim's thought and has produced many spiritual Sufis who further strengthen the faith of Muslims across the literary world. The great idea of education was promoted by every caliphate and vizier; it was the main priority in every household. Every field of science, medicine and art blossomed during this period of time but it is now referred to as the Islamic Golden Age.

Today what is known as Iran –Persia, is home to one of the world's oldest continuous civilizations. There was a time when ancient Persian civilization was in fact the most powerful empire in the world. Persians conquered lands that covered over two million square miles. From the southern portions of Egypt to parts of Greece and then east to parts of India, the Persian Empire was known for its military strength and its wise rulers.

The earliest archaeological artefacts in Iran were found in the Kashafrud and Garnj Par sites that are thought to date back to 100,000 years ago in the Middle Palaeolithic. There are also 10,000-year-old human and animal figurines from Teppe Sarab in Kermanshah province among the many other ancient artefacts. Iran is home to a major, and one of the world's oldest, continuous civilizations with historical and urban settlement dating back to 4000BC.

Persian civilization was also very rich in its culture and many achievements. The Greek historian, Hegel, names the Persians as the first historical people. The Medes are credited with the foundations of Iran as a nation and empire and established the Iranian empire the largest of its day until Cyrus the Great established a unified empire of the Medes and Persian leading to the Achaemenian empire c 550-330 BC.

Cyrus the Great overthrew in turn the Median Empire, Lydian Empire and the Neo Babylonian Empire, creating an empire far larger than Assyria. He was better able, through more benign policies to reconcile his subjects to Persian rule for many years. The Persian king was also known as the king of kings. Under Cyrus the Great and Darius the Great, the Persian empire eventually became the largest empire in human history. Until that point, ruling and serving its vast population with policies based on equality, justice and fairness, a transparent system of administration which was maintained with ruling fear of swift accountably through the designated vizier. Ruling over most of the known world, as well as spanning three continents, namely Europe, Asia, and Africa. Their greatest achievement was the empire itself. The Persian Empire represented the world's first superpower that was based on a model of tolerance and respect for other religions. Zoroastrianism was the official religion of the Achaemenes dynasty. It was reconstructed as the official religion of the Sassanid dynasty. The name Zoroaster is derived from a Greek mangling of the name Zarathustra, a prophet like figure who lived at the time before 600 BCE. Zoroastrianism is one of the world's oldest religions combining a cosmogonic dualism and eschatological monotheism in a manner unique amongst the major religion of the world. It was founded by the Zoroaster in ancient Iran approximately 3500 years ago.

In order to have some knowledge of this ancient religion, here are some keys terms that provide us with some understanding of this religion. *Adur or Atar*, Sacred fire. All fire is considered purified and is ritually tended in temples and some holy places. *Ahura Mazda* The wise lord, the creator God later Ohrmazd, *Amesha Spentas* The seven holy Immortals, regarded as offshoots or emanations of God. *Angra Mainyu* the hostile spirit, source of all evil, destined eventually to be overcome by Ahura Mazda later Ahriman.*Bundahishn* means the creation of the world arising out of war between the Good and Evil Spirits. *Frashokereti* The act of creation, the occasion of resurrection and of the final judgment. *Fravashis* the eternal spirit of human beings, which exist in heaven rather like angels, the implication is that humans have freely chosen to assume material form.

Manthras, words of power prayer drawn mainly from the earliest scriptures attributed to Zarathusra. These beliefs contain some aspects of the truth of a creator at least, which may have been influenced by another religion of its time.

(In Khorasan in north-eastern Iran, a 10th century Iranian nobleman brought together four Zoroastrian priests to transcribe Sassanid-era Middle Persian work titled *Book of the lord* from Pahlavi script to Arabic script. This transcription which remained in Middle Persian prose, was completed in 957 and subsequently the basis for Firdausi *Book of kings* it became enormously popular). Sasanians who governed Iran for almost 1000 years once again the leading power in the world only this time amongst the arch rivals the Romans and successive Byzantine Empire.

Once a major superpower, having conquered far and wide, becoming a great empire, it has also endured many years of conflicts, wars and invasions, first by Greeks, Arabs Turks and the Mongols. Alexander the Great defeated Darius III in the battle of Granicus, Issus, and Gaugamela. A chapter of Iran's history followed, after roughly six hundred years of conflict with the Roman Empire, during this time the Sassanian and Romano-Byzantine armies clashed for influence in Anatolia, the western Caucasus modern day

Georgia Abkhazia, Mesopotamia, Armenia and the Levant. Under Justinian I, the war came to an uneasy peace payment of tribute to the Sassanians. After many gains, Sasanians were defeated at Issus, Constantinople and Nineveh, resulting in peace. With the conclusion of the over 700 years lasting Roman Persian wars.

The advent of true faith in 600 BC when the Prophet Mohammed began to preach publicly advocating the worship of a single God, Muslims began conquests outside Arabia and gained Byzantine territory with the capture of Damascus. Egypt fell to the Muslims and by 650 BC the Muslims continue the conquest and the Arabs gain Persia. The Islamization of Iran was to yield deep transformations with cultural scientific and political structure of Iran's society. The unique Persian literature, philosophy, medicine and art became major elements of a newly forming Muslim civilization. Inheriting a heritage of thousands of year's civilization and being at the crossroads of the major cultural highways contributed to Persia emerging as what has culminated into the Islamic golden age. During this period, hundreds of scholars and scientists vastly contributed to technology, science and medicine, later influencing the rise of European science during the Renaissance. The most important scholars of almost all the Islamic sects and schools of thought were Persian or lived in Iran, including the most notable and reliable Hadith collectors like Imam Muslim and Imam Bukhari. He was born on 13th Shawwal in the year 194 AH (Muslim calendar) He laboured night and day, collected and memorize thousands of Hadiths and chose approximately 7275 of which there is no doubt about their authenticity. It has been unanimously agreed by all the Islamic religious scholars that Imam Bukhari's work is the most authentic of all the works in Hadith literature put together. To this day his work is considered to be, "The most authentic book after the book of Allah (Al –Quran) is sahih Al- Bukhari. For the Muslims that follow the true religion of Islam by accepting the word of God holy Quran and put in practice Al Bukhari's hadiths the teaching of Prophet Muhammed."

Iran enjoyed a cultural and scientific renaissance largely attributed to a brilliant Iranian vizier, Nizam al Mulk, and the leader of the time, Malik Shah 1072-1092, established the observatory where Omar Khayyam did much of his experimentation for a new calendar and they built religious schools in all major towns. They brought Abu Hamid Ghazzali, one the greatest Islamic theologians. He was born in 450 A.H. (1058 A.D) in the village Taberan in the district of Taus in Persia. He was the leader in Islam's supreme encounter with Greek Philosophy – that encounter from which Islamic theology emerged victorious and enriched and in which Arabic neoplatonism received a blow from which it did not recover. He saved Islam from the currents and cross currents of devilish thoughts and pagan ideas that in perceptibly entered into Islam and clearly showed their fallacies and misconceptions.

For this reason, he was given the title of Hujjatul Islam – proof of Islam. His four volume book*, Ihya Ulum-id-din* – the revival of religious science is a master piece. A scholar of that time, Shaikh Abu Mohammed said, "If all the lights of knowledge of the world are extinguished they can be revived from his work of Ihya Ulum-id-din. "

Also, the most revered Shaikh Abd-Al-Qadir Al Jilani was born in the Iranian district of Gilan south of the Caspian Sea in A.H. 470/1077-8 CE. Often referred to as the sultan of saints his sixty-two discourses from his book titled *The Sublime Revelation* are his spoken words over a 1000 years ago, still transcends the time and place in which they were recorded to the span of centuries without difficulty. His talks contain the most beautiful oratory the world has ever known. He used to mesmerise his audience with his presence and awe, as he stated in one his sermons at his schoolhouse,

" I am no ordinary preacher "I only utter what God makes me utter. At his hand, thousands of males and females from every walk life from far and wide, freely accepted the true religion of Islam. His true spoken words will continue to provide true guidance to all mankind until time immemorial. It is rightly said of him he was born in love, grew in perfection, and met his lord in the perfection of love. His memorable saying and wise teaching are rightly titled in his book as pearls of wisdom.

Great contributions and guidance with the light of inspiration continued in Persia over the centuries by the six greatest classical poets of Persia, Firdausi , Nizami , Sadi, Hafiz, Jami, and more commonly known in the literary world of today, Jalal ad din Rumi, who was born in 1207 in the northern Persian province of Khorasan. He came from a family of preachers and men of religion. He underwent spiritual revolution in 1244 after meeting Shams al din of Tabriz. Rumi's *The Mathnawi* his famous work of six volumes, are 25,700 verses of Persian poetry mostly inspired by true Islamic Hadiths and the holy Quran. He concentrates on the spiritual message of the scriptures as he reflects through his discourses, remembering and advocating the Islamic laws with the cloak of Sufiism, always representing the truth. Rumi is remembered as a Sufi poet, the author of prolific outpouring of verses, he continues to inspire men and women in the east and the west over seven hundred years later and his teachings resonate with readers of all faiths and creeds. He will always be considered as a national treasure of Persia. Even today, he is the bestselling poet in the United States of America. His monumental works continue to inspire religious scholars across the globe, his short stories and references are full of wisdom, always shining light and guiding the reader, to the noble and virtuous qualities of human nature within. Also reminding the reader of the pitfalls of surrendering of "self" to selfish passions and desires – our common human weakness to, greed, lust, eminence, dominance, praise and control.

Iran was no exception to selfish human nature in its history, it did fall prey from time to time to the hungry men pursuing their desires driven by their ultra-egos, some looking for power, control or dominance, while others were looking to conquer land or simply to rule it. The Mongol invasion 1219-1221 was disastrous for Iranians. The Mongol invaders were eventually converted to Islam and accepted the culture of Iran. The Mongol destruction of the Islamic heartland marked a major change of direction for the region. Much of the six centuries of Islamic scholarship, culture and infrastructure was destroyed and invaders burned libraries and replaced mosques and Buddhist temples. The Mongols killed many civilians. Destroyed qanat irrigation systems and patterns of relatively continuous settlements, destroying rare, isolated cities. A large number of people, particularly males were killed between 1220 and 1258, the total population of Iran may have dropped from 2,500,000 to 250,000 as a result of mass extermination and famine.

Iran's history is rich with the records of rule of many dynasties and Shas that brought it prosperity over the centuries of its existence. Iran has always managed to continually preserve its national identity through the centuries and had developed as a distinct political and cultural entity, and has preserved its own language. The spread of Islam in Iran took place during 8th to 10th century and led to the decline of Zoroastrian religion in Persia as well as many of its dependencies. However, the achievements of the previous Persian civilizations were not lost but were to a great extent absorbed by the new Islamic policy and civilization. Iran was once again reunified as an independent state in 1501 by the Safavid dynasty, which established Shia Islam as the official religion of their empire marking one of the most important turning points in the history of Islam. Functioning again as a leading power this time amongst their neighbouring Ottoman arch-rivals for centuries, Iran had been a monarchy ruled by a shah or emperor, almost without interruptions from 1501 until the 1979 Iranian revolution when Iran officially became an Islamic republic on 1 April 1979.

The **Roman civilization** in the world's history began during 800 BC. Their foundations with its name Roma, are full of myth and legend. According to the myth, the city of Rome was founded on 21 April 753 BC by twin brothers Romulus and Remus who descended from the Trojan prince Aeneas. Also a reference of Rome's existence is found in the world history books, it is recorded as a major event that took place in 400 BC, when the Celts sacked Rome but quickly withdrew. In the beginning Rome was a small city state on the Tiber, Rome expanded relentlessly after 400 BC, by 250 BC the romans controlled most of Italy and were locked in struggle with Carthage for mastery of the western Mediterranean. A century later, Carthage lay in ruins, and Roman forces had pushed through Greece into Asia Minor. Military success heightened political tensions in Rome; in 45 BC, Julius Caesar capitalized on his triumph by seizing absolute power. His successors extended the empire until it reached its zenith early in the second century AD, lower Mesopotamia remained a contested area between the Romans and the Parthians. Ancient Rome was an Italic civilization that began on the Italian peninsula in the 8th century BC located along the Mediterranean Sea and centred on the city of Rome. It expanded to become one of the largest empires in the ancient world with an estimated 50 to 90 million inhabitants approximately 20% of the world's population covering 6.5 million square kilometres during it height between the first and second centuries AD. In its 1200 years of existence, Roman civilization changed from monarchy to a republic and to an autocratic empire. Through conquest and assimilation, it came to dominate southern and western Europe, Asia Minor, and North Africa. The supremacy of Caesar's Rome was maintained by well-disciplined and highly organized forces of professional soldiers called legionaries. A recruit enlisted for twenty-five years and after an arduous training joined one of twenty-eight legions that formed the backbone of the Roman army. Ancient Roman society has contributed to modern government, law, politics, engineering, art, literature, architecture, technology, warfare, religion, language, and society. A highly developed civilization, Rome professionalized and expanded its military and created a system of government called SPQR, Senates Populous Que Romanus- res publics, now considered in some ways as the inspiration to the formations of modern republics.

It achieved impressive technological and architectural feats such as the construction of an extensive system of aqueducts and roads and large monuments, palaces and public facilities.

Around 120 AD, the Emperor Hadrian, a cultivated man with a great passion for architecture, commissioned a building that would stand as a monument to the highest aspiration of imperial Rome, known as the Pantheon or place of all gods, the structure was a roofed rotunda, ringed with seven recesses, possibly shrines for deities associated with the heavens such as Mars, Mercury, Venus and Jupiter. The dome that capped the hall was symbolic of the firmament through its open eye or oculus the suns ray gilded the marble floor.

The native language of the Rome was Latin, an Italic language, the grammar of which relies little on word order conveying meaning through a system of affixes attached to word stems. While Latin remained the main written language of the Roman Empire, Greek came to be the language spoken by the well-educated elites as most of the literature studied by the Romans was written in Greek. The expansions of the

Roman Empire spread Latin throughout Europe, it evolved into dialects in different locations. In the early Republic, there were no public schools, so the boys were taught to read and write by their parents or educated salves called Pedagogy usually of Greek origin. The primary aim of education during this period was to train young men in agriculture, warfare, and public affairs (Roman traditions).

The sons of nobles were apprenticed to prominent political figures at the age of sixteen and campaigned with the army from the age of seventeen. Roman society was largely viewed as hierarchical with slaves at the bottom, freemen above them and free born citizens at the top. Also, it was based on ancestry and heritage, anyone who could count a consul as his ancestor was a noble, a man who was to his family to hold consulship such as Marius or Cicero.

The basic units of Roman society were household and families. The household included the head, usually the father his wife, children and relatives. The power of the head of the household was supreme, he could force marriage for money, sell his children into slavery, claim his dependents property as his own and even had the right to punish or kill family members. Roman religion concerning the gods was made up not of written narratives but rather of complex interrelation between gods and humans. Unlike Greek mythology, they were not personified but vaguely defined sacred spirits called numina. Romans also believed that every person, place or thing had its own genius or divine soul. During the Roman republic, Roman religion was organized under a strict system of priestly offices which were held by men of senatorial rank. As contact with the Greeks increased, the old Roman gods became increasingly associated with Greek gods. Thus Jupiter was perceived to be the same deity as Zeus, Mars became associated with Aries and Neptune with Poseidon. The Roman gods also assumed the attributes and mythologies of these Greek gods. Under the Empire, the Romans absorbed the mythologies of their conquered subjects, often leading to situations in which the temples and priests of traditional Italian deities existed side by side with those foreign gods.

Beginning with Emperor Nero in the 1st century AD, Roman official policy towards Christianity was negative and at some points, simply being a Christian could be punishable by death. Under Emperor Diocletian, the persecution of Christians reached its peak. However, it became an officially supported religion in the Roman state under Diocletian's successor Constantine 1. In 312 he defeated Maxentius at the battle of the Milvian Bridge and became sole emperor of both the Western and Eastern Empires ruling from 306- 337 CE. Believing that Jesus Christ was responsible for his victory Constantine initiated a series of laws such as Edict of Milan 317 CE, which mandated religious tolerance throughout the empire. He presided over the gathering to codify the faith and decide on important issues such as the divinity of Jesus and which manuscripts would be collected to form the book known today as The Bible.

According to *Time-line History of the World,* the chronology of major events refers:

0-AD as when Christ is born. Augustus dies, his stepson Tiberius succeeds him, Caligula succeeds Tiberius, and Claudius becomes emperor and conquers Britain. AD 50 Nero accedes to the throne, Rome burns, giving Nero an excuse to begin the persecutions of Christians. Mount Vesuvius erupts and buries Pompeii and Herculaneum. Under Trajan, the empire reaches its greatest extent. In AD 100, Hadrian suppresses the revolt of the Jews and denies them access to Jerusalem. During 150, Marcus Aurelius, who would be called the last good emperor who ruled for nineteen years, after which the empire begins its decline. Edward Gibbon wrote in his *Decline and Fall of the Roman Empire,* "After a diligent inquiry I can discern four principal causes of the ruin of Rome which continued to operate in a period of more than thousand years. Firstly the injuries of time and nature, secondly the hostile attacks of the barbarians and Christians, thirdly the use and abuse of the materials, fourthly the domestic quarrels of the Romans."

Now, a great part of Roman history remains a great credit, to the English writer,

Edward Gibbon born on 27 April 1737 died 16th 1794. He remains a classic historian whose monumental works of six volumes of history, on the decline and fall of the Roman Empire, is a masterpiece. With his noble English and supreme literary skill and ambition, he provides the reader with historical accuracy of a once great empire, the organization of his work is fascinating, his years of labour is seen as a work of genius by some and will remain superior.

The art of man is able to construct a monument that outlives the narrow span of his own mortal life. The historians will continue to produce different factors to support their theories about the fall of the Roman Empire, like, corruption, disloyalty or disease, or inequality or shameful immorality, or the vastness of the empire being too big to govern, or even

Christianity. With all these true findings, they would all be referring to some parts of all these elements that actually did contribute and caused of the downfall of the Romans. It also leaves the reader to reach their own conclusions, on each of the kings, caesars, emperors and dictators that ruled the empire. They were all prone to human weaknesses of passion and selfish desires, eminence, pride, and show. A majority of them simply ruled to impress and to be remembered as great and glorious, a part combination of these weaknesses was the fall of each ruler and the decline of their empire. They did not serve in the publics' best interest by not maintaining divine rule and justice but ruled with their own doctrines that gave little importance to human life. They simply ignored their creator and his messengers who brought the true message from God.

Then evil was the end of those who did evil because they denied the revelations , proofs , evidence , lessons and signs from God's Messengers and make mockery of them[82]

The readers can form their own opinion of Roman's values, principles and beliefs from the brief description provided with the five main points when, where, what they believed and what they practiced and what was their outcome. Some factual records of Roman history by different historians may lead to disagreement or inspire a new discussions and even heated debate, but on each occasion and in every exchange the participants would have to remind themselves that it was all in the past, some aspect of which

---

[82] Quran(30:10)

cannot be physically verified. But, the following information is not just for the elite or the privileged few, it is commonly accessible because it is not locked up in a library's vault or stored and guarded in a religious monument.

It is a book to benefit all humans, it is the light and true guidance for all mankind, will remain so till the end of time – The Holy Quran.

And this Quran is not such as could ever be produced by other than Allah (the lord of heavens an the earth) but it is a confirmation of the revelations which was before it Tura and Gospel and a full explanation book (Law decreed for mankind) wherein there is no doubt from the Lord of mankind and jinn and all that exists[83]

Say, "If all the mankind and jinn were together to produce the like of this Quran they could not produce the like thereof, even if they help one another[84]

Now living in the modern age of information, we form our opinions based on our knowledge and experience. The following is a reminder from the creator of all the ancient civilizations and their final outcome.

Do they not travel in the land, and see what the end of those before them was?

They were superior in strength and they tilled the earth and populated it in greater numbers than these pagans have done, there came to them their messengers with clear proof

---

[83] Quran(10:37)
[84] Quran(17:88)

surely Allah wronged them not but they used to wrong themselves[85]

In the following eight verses (of surah Rum 613 AD) of the holy Quran, these revelations to prophet Muhammed directly address the fate of the Romans and the Persians and the subsequent success of the Muslims with the promise of God, and reminding mankind of their folly of only giving importance to this material world and denying meeting their lord. These revelations are from God. They cannot be referred to like the past written by a historian, these facts are not open to discussions or different interpretations.

The Romans have been defeated[86]

In the nearest land, Syria, Iraq, Jordan and Palestine and after their defeat will be Victorious[87]

Within three to nine years. The decision of the matter, before and after (these events) is only with Allah, (before the defeat of the Romans by the Persians and after the defeat of the Persians by the Romans) and on that day the believers (Muslims) will rejoice at the victory given by Allah to the Roman against the Persians[88]

With the help of Allah He helps whom he wills and he is almighty and merciful [89]

---

[85] Quran(30:9)
[86] Quran(30:2)
[87] Quran(30:3)
[88] Quran(30:4)
[89] Quran(30:5)

It is a promise of Allah will give victory to the romans against the Persians and Allah fails not in his promise but most men know not[90]

They know only the outside appearance of the life of this world (the matters of their livelihood like irrigating or sowing or reaping) and they are heedless of the hereafter.[91]

Do they not think deeply (in their own selves) about themselves (how Allah created them from nothing and similarly he will resurrect them) Allah has created not the heavens and the earth and all that is between them, except with truth and form an appointed term. And indeed many of mankind deny the meeting with their lord[92]

For many centuries, man has tried to understand God's creations, the stars and planets sometimes without drawing any benefit from the divine revelations which are a permanent reminder for men of understanding.

The creation of the heavens and the earth is indeed greater than the creation of mankind, most men know not[93]

And He it is who has created the night and the day, and the sun and the moon, each in an orbit floating.[94]

---

[90] Quran(30:6)
[91] Quran(30:7)
[92] Quran(30:8)
[93] Quran(40:57)
[94] Quran(21:330

Understanding the Universe

One of man's earliest interest in astronomy began with **Aristotle** (384- 322 BC), a Philosopher, scientist, and physician, who taught that the Earth is the centre of the eternal universe, that everything below the orbit of the moon is made up of earth, air, fire, and water subject to generation, destruction and qualitative change, and rectilinear motions and that everything above the orbit of the moon is made of ether and never changes but is subject to circular motion.

Ptolemy (90-168 AD) astronomer and geographer – The Ptolemaic bodies (stars) into scientific form. Earth is the centre of the universe with the stars revolving around it. In the ether above the atmosphere, are seven concentric spheres each containing a planet and an eighth containing the fixed stars? It predicted the position of the stars to within one degree of accuracy.

Nicolaus Copernicus (1473- 1543) founder of modern astronomy deeply troubled by Ptolemy's assertion that the earth was the centre of the universe, started mathematical explanations of the sun being the centre of the universe, but unwilling to publish for the fear of the church establishment. 1543, by now old and ill he was reluctantly persuaded by his pupil, Rheticus to finally publish his theories on the revaluations on the heavenly spheres. He dedicated the work to Pope Paul III. Copernicus received his copy on his deathbed. The book scandalized the establishment and was immediately banned by the Catholic Church and placed on the list of forbidden books, where it remained until 1853.

Galileo Galilei 1564- 1642 philosopher and mathematician. 1604 demonstrated the movement of stars.1610, produced his refracting telescope The Mountains of the moon, Jupiter, satellites and the stars in the Milky Way were seen clearly for the first time. In 1633, he was tried for heresy in Rome for defending Copernicus' systems.

Isaac Newton 1642-1727 scientist, mathematician and discoverer of gravity also studied the reflection of sunlight through a prism. Newton's work was recognized at once as a vindication of the belief that nature worked through laws and the key to those laws was the language of mathematics. No one could deny the proof that Newton had provided of the universality of gravity. But at the same time there was a mystery at the heart of his work for nowhere was there even a hint at what gravity was and how it could operate across empty space. To this day, no particle or ray or wave of gravity has ever been discovered although its laws are irrefutable.

Some people may still have the view that his work has immense philosophical implications giving rise to the image that the universe is a miraculous mechanism, a vast clock machine that has been set in motion by its creator. That functions by immutable and perfect laws. God was to be seen in the faultless eternal working of his creation. In order to describe the mechanics of the universe, three basic factors are required, space, time and mass.

It was **Albert Einstein** 1879- 1955, who showed that the three are related to each other in ways that had never been truly understood. 1905, published theories on relativity which won him world-wide acclaim. The universe is composed of Matter, Space, and Time and explained how all three are interdependent. As without Matter, there is no absolute space or time, in the same way a room is only defined by the four walls which enclose it. This means that space and time are fluid and have properties which can change under different conditions. Einstein takes us into the realms of the atom, the speed of light and the depths of the cosmos. The last thirty years of his life were spent in search of a unified field theory "that would embrace gravity and electromagnetism the cosmos and the atom." He was deeply distrustful of quantum physics and felt that it must be possible to build a model of physical reality as it is just a mere probability system. His criticism of quantum theory, "That God does not play dice with the universe," has become famous. Perhaps Niels Bohr's reply deserves equal weight that, "We cannot tell God how to organise the universe."

These are only some of the great men of understanding of our recent times whose great discoveries have helped us to have a better understanding of the world we live in. Their passionate devotions and endeavours to know the truth have changed the way we perceive realty and the world around us. Their great achievements laid the basis and foundation of universal laws of travelling in space, which has inspired men to take greater leaps of discovery. The staggering advance achieved with digital computer technology has made so many inventions possible, such as landing on the moon.

We all have learnt the planet Earth is one of the eight which orbit around the central star, the Sun. In our solar system Earth is the third planet in terms of distance from the sun, Mercury is the closest, with Venus next. Further are Mars, Jupiter, Saturn, Neptune and Pluto. Jupiter is the largest planet in our solar system with the diameter of 89,000 miles compared to Earth's 8,000 miles. Earth orbits around the sun at 100,000 Kilometre per hour covering over 900,000,000 kilometres in 365 days. As it orbits, it is also spinning round on its axis's, in twenty-four hours we experience the creations, the wonder of night and day. The spin of the earth not only gives us the natural phenomena of night and day, which is crucial for our existence. It is always spinning on it axis with an important 23% tilt, which creates and give us different seasons in different parts of the world at different times which are a phenomena in itself. The seasonal change is imperative for all life on earth to exist, without it, all life would end. The cold North Pole, the hot deserts and tropical growth, all influence and contribute to the change and manipulate our weather. The Earth's spin controls the major weather related events like storms, hurricanes, tsunamis and floods. All natural events which are controlled by our creator.

And in the alternation of night and day and the provision (rain) that Allah sends down from the sky, and revives therewith the earth after its death, and in the turning about the winds (i.e. sometimes towards the east or north, sometimes towards the south or west sometimes

bringing glad tidings of rain and sometimes bringing the torment) Are the signs for a people who understand?[95]

Allah causes the night and the day to succeed each other truly in this in lesson for those who have insight[96]

Edwin Powell Hubble 1889-1953 Astronomer and the founder of modern cosmology discovered that spiral nebulas are an independent stellar system, studied the velocity of galaxies.

In 1929, he published his discovery concerning the expansion of the universe. Galaxies recede at a speed that increases with distance; the Hubble constant is a measure of this rate.

Before mankind could even understand the structure of the universe, we are faced with grasping its infinite size. In trying to observe and have some understanding of the universe the average person in overwhelmed by its sheer size. We glibly refer to objects located many light years away from earth and this gives us reassuring units to measure. When it is realised that light travels 186,000 miles per second, the distance travelled in one year is unimaginable. Even in one day, light travels over 16 billion miles. When we talk about the object being billions of light years away, the figures are beyond average comprehension.

A galaxy is a discrete concentration of numerous stars separated from similar formations by huge distances. A single galaxy can contain literally billions of stars and can stretch across thousands of light-years in space. When Harlow

---

[95] Quran(45:5)
[96] Quran(4:44)

Shepley announced in 1917 his finding that our Galaxy, the Milky Way, must have a diameter of approximately 300,000 light-years, it was a unique observation. Now we also learn from devoted astronomers, the nearest galaxy to the Milky Way is the Andromeda galaxy there are some 200 galaxies grouped together as clusters. It is estimated that the total mass of all the stars and other bodies in the group is equal to 500 billion suns. The size of the cosmos is truly beyond human comprehension. There is only one creator who has laid claim to the creation of this infinite universe.

Fourteen hundred years ago, the Creator sent the Prophet Muhammad to mankind and in the Holy Quran his revelations state:

And if all the trees on the earth were pens and the sea (were ink wherewith to write) with seven seas behind it to add to its supply yet the words of Allah would not be exhausted verily Allah is All Mighty, All wise.[97]

Conclusion

From an early age, we are taught by our parents and guardians to always be physically clean and presentable. It is an important part of our personality. When we behave according and appropriately, in any given situation, we are considered to have good manners.

When we respond with our cognitive experiences we are considered to be competent and wise. When we apply our learning, education and skills we are considered to be

[97] Quran (31:27)

intelligent, all these traits contribute in forming our personality.

Naturally, we use our sense perceptions to fulfil our immediate needs and natural desires to maintain life. To appreciate how these senses are formed, we need to have knowledge to understand their wonderful qualities and amazing limits.

It is also important to understand our inner-self; its understanding can help us to bring a positive change to our personality. Knowledge about our perceptions, self-awareness consciousness, our values, faith in self and God are all important for every personality.

In this book the following sections provide useful information on what is **self**, the importance of **know thyself**, the realising of **self-awareness,** the acknowledgment of **spirit-soul,** the formation and the functions of the **brain,** the importance of our **sense perceptions** and significance of our **heart,** and the pivotal role our **conscience** and **faith** play in our lives to make important decisions. How all our faculties, attributes, learnings and experiences, all jointly contribute to form our **personality**. The four natural elements of human nature are greed, lust or evil and saintly desires. If any one of these elements dominate over the others, it would give shape to that personality. The importance of faith in **self** and **God,** which needs to be an integral part of life. The divine revelation provides true knowledge and understanding to obtain internal peace and contentment. These revelations remind us of the calamities that destroyed the **ancient civilizations,** due to the ignorance of the divine revelations, and the defiance and rejection of truth to belief in one true God and his messengers.

To benefit the reader, with the help of science, psychology, philosophy, and history and divine revelations some information is presented. All to assist and help the reader to establish a clear understanding of himself, their faith, values and purpose in life – all can be achieved by gaining a better understanding and learning from true knowledge.